Penguin Books
SLEEP

Rod Usher is a journalist and author. He has
worked overseas for the BBC, the *Times* and
the *Sunday Times*. His other books are
Above Water and *Images of Our Time*. He is
now working for the *Age* in Melbourne.

Ron Tandberg works for the *Age*, and the
Sydney Morning Herald. His cartoons have
won him no fewer than seven Walkley
Awards, the highest honour in Australian
journalism, and have filled several books.

SLEEP

Things That Happen in the Night

Illustrations by Ron Tandberg

ROD USHER

Penguin Books

Penguin Books Australia Ltd,
487 Maroondah Highway, PO Box 257
Ringwood, Victoria 3134, Australia
Penguin Books Ltd,
Harmondsworth, Middlesex, England
Penguin Books,
40 West 23rd Street, New York, NY 10010, USA
Penguin Books Canada Ltd,
2801 John Street, Markham, Ontario, Canada L3R 1B4
Penguin Books (NZ) Ltd,
182-190 Wairau Road, Auckland 10, New Zealand

First published by Penguin Books Australia, 1986

Typeset in Palatino and Futura Book by Leader Composition Pty Ltd.
Made and printed in Australia by The Dominion Press-Hedges & Bell.

Usher, Rod.
Sleep, things that happen in the night.

ISBN 0 14 008786 9 (pbk.).

1. Sleep. 2. Sleep – Physiological aspects. 3. Dreams.
I. Tandberg, Ron, 1943- . II. Title.

154.6

To my mother, Margaret

CONTENTS

THINGS THAT HAPPEN IN THE NIGHT

SLEEP is a blessed funny thing. Blessed because it is beyond money. It is 'the poor man's wealth, the prisoner's release', as Sir Philip Sidney wrote more than 400 years ago. Funny because, as Freud said, 'Anyone who when he was awake behaved in the sort of way that is shown in situations in dreams would be considered insane.'

Sleep can be frightening; Hamlet might have said, 'To sleep perchance to scream.' And it can be enlightening, both the sewing machine and the plot for *Dr Jekyll and Mr Hyde* having been dream-inspired. We walk in it, talk in it, or snort like a truffle-hunting pig in it. Worse than anything we might do in our sleep is the prospect of waiting for it to come when it won't, only to be wrenched jangling from it by an alarm when we've found it.

There can also be a simplicity to sleep that is singularly beautiful. One woman wrote to me about a dream she had when she was ten in which she had been playing in her garden with some fairies. Time came for them to leave but so enchanted was she with their games that she tried to follow them. The girl awoke standing on her dressing table trying to climb into the mirror above it.

Sleep can strain marriage. One woman wrote of waking in a tight headlock. She was not dreaming. It was very real and was being applied by her loving husband as he dreamt.

On average we spend twenty-two years of our lives asleep. We know a lot more about it than we used to but, in many ways, it is as much a mystery as the black holes of outer space.

This book aims to take a peek under sleep's covers. My thanks to all who let me into their beds, so to speak, and to the doctors, psychologists and other sleep researchers who aided and abetted.

THE NEED

ADAM SLEPT. So did Eve. Then they slept together . . . and today there are nearly five billion of us! Of course just sleeping with someone has never produced a baby. Procreation is a wide awake business. But sleeping is suitably mysterious and benign to be used as a euphemism for sex.

Sleeping – together or alone – is a bigger thing than procreation. The latter, no matter how imperative, is an option. The former ranks with breathing, water and bread as one of life's essentials. Just as there is clean and polluted air, sparkling and slimy water, fresh and stale bread, so there is good and bad sleep.

What sorts sleep from life's other essentials is that it is very hard to pin down. We all know about respiration and nutrition, and there are few other bodily functions and conditions that have not been fully measured and analysed. But once we shut our eyes the scientists are still pretty much in the dark.

Sleep researchers have made enormous advances since the 1950s when it was learned that sleep happens in definable stages, its two most obvious forms being REM, the rapid eye movement that is associated with dreaming, and non-REM, or non-rapid eye movement sleep, which is not. But despite these advances, the first and most obvious question – why do we sleep – has not been answered. This is not necessarily a bad thing. As Dante said in *Inferno:* 'It pleases me as much to doubt as to know.'

One of the pioneers of modern sleep research, Dr William Dement (a co-discoverer of REM and non-REM sleep), after decades at it, still speaks of sleep with a sense of awe: 'Because sleep occurs during the dark hours when man is least able to cope with his environment, and because man asleep is not alert to the dangers of the outer world, sleep is a state of vulnerability. It is necessary to seek a place of refuge in which to sleep. A troop of baboons has its tree, the wolf has its den; primitive man had his cave or his hut, and we have our bedrooms. Having constructed a safe place to sleep, man is able to use the word "home".'

The need to curl up within our fortress homes, heads propped on soft bags, between large squares of cotton and then wool, on top of rectangles stuffed with kapok, tensioned with springs or filled with water, is unique to each of us. A 'good night's sleep' is something in the closed eyes of the beholder. Clearly, some need more than others. Twenty-five years ago, Dr Dement monitored the attempt of an American high school student named Randy Gardner to set a record for going without sleep and verified that Randy stayed awake eleven days – 264 hours and twelve minutes, to be precise.

At the other end of the scale, some people fall asleep anywhere, literally. They can be walking along, talking normally, then fall to the ground, sound asleep as a baby with a full belly.

My interest in sleep began when I worked with such a person at the BBC in London in 1970. It is not the sort of place you would expect to find a sleepyhead, a newsroom broadcasting twenty-four hours a day in forty languages to all parts of the world. As a junior sub-editor, I would help to compile bulletin items from material that poured in from the main news agencies and from the BBC's overseas correspondents. These items would then go to a more senior sub-editor for checking and re-editing, then to a duty editor, who would have another look, himself under the overviewing eye of a senior duty editor. Once everybody was satisfied, the item, which might be as short as five or six lines on a page, would be set down afresh by a fast typist. She would bring it back to the original sub-editor to ensure there were no mistakes and at last it would be ready for translation into tongues such as Swahili or Vietnamese or to be read for the World Service by one of those inimitably British BBC voices. All of which may be reinforcing your respect for the journalistic standards of the BBC, but what has it got to do with sleep? Well, I had not been there long when I noticed that one of the aforesaid typists, a small, dumpy woman of about thirty, would often fall asleep right in the middle of hitting her keyboard. One minute she'd be all wakeful dexterity, the next she would be like the wheelchair corpse in 'Psycho', head slumped on her breast, arms limp at her sides. A few minutes later, her head would jerk back, her shoulders would straighten, and she would resume the news item where she left off.

I remember asking one of my English colleagues what was wrong with this unfortunate young woman. With typical English reserve and the slightly raised eyebrow that is offered the brash Antipodean, he replied: 'Oh, she does that all the time.' His response to it, like the rest of the staff, was total politeness and no questions asked. If a news item was needed at top speed to be rushed into the studio as the bulletin was being read, they didn't give it to this typist.

Today, knowing a little more about sleep than I did then, I could guess that the poor woman was probably a sufferer of narcolepsy, a debilitating disorder that plunges its victims into deep sleep at any time. Instead of the normal stages of drowsiness and physical relaxation, the blurred line between wakefulness and sleep, a sufferer of narcolepsy can drop straight into sudden slumber while talking, walking, even making love. Falling asleep can became painfully literal.

I also now know why some journalists at the BBC would choose to work dawn shifts. For most of us, 'dawns' – starting at 11 pm and finishing at 7 am – were a part of the job that had to be fitted into the system because we broadcast over many time zones. Typically we would work three day shifts, three afternoon-evening shifts and then have three days off. But when the rosters went up you'd find that two or three dawns would be woven into each shift pattern. I hated them; they always made me feel slightly jetlagged and somehow cheated. I'd get back home wide awake as the family was breakfasting, then wrestle with sleep with the curtains drawn. Alternatively I'd go and drink Guinness morosely in one of the early opening pubs near Covent Garden market.

A minority of my sallow-faced colleagues, however, would work permanent dawns, and would complain bitterly if it was suggested that they transfer to daylight hours or even to the afternoon-evening shift. To them light meant sleep, dark meant work; like moles and owls they were at their best at night.

But apart from the extremes of Randy Gardner and the BBC typist, and the slightly less odd dawn brigade, what about the common or garden sleeper? Why does he or she do it? What's the biological, evolutionary dictate that makes us say, 'Now I lay me down to sleep'?

The same question can be put another way. Sleep can be seen as the norm and wakefulness as the aberration, simply a reaction to muscular and mental activity. Switch off the senses and the cerebral circuitry and the body will resort to somnolence, like a car with the key turned off. The idea that the brain's natural state may be 'off' rather than 'on' has been postulated by many scientists, including William Dement's mentor and one of the father figures of modern sleep research, Dr Nathaniel Kleitman. Certainly in the exaggerated case of Randy Gardner it was constant physical stimulation, such as playing pinball machines, that enabled him to stave off sleep for so long.

On the other hand, and this is not necessarily a contradiction, if you remove just some of the sources of human stimulation, you can get indications that wakefulness is the natural state. Tests on US navy recruits gave a clue to this. The volunteers were each put into a dark, sound-proofed room for seven days (they had chemical toilets and food supplies to fumble with) and steadily the time they spent sleeping dropped to an average of less than six hours a day by the end.

It is easy to dismiss such ideas as inconclusive hairsplitting and to assume that we obviously sleep for restoration, to recharge the batteries. But this is hard to prove.

One prominent sleep researcher who has queried the restoration theory is Dr Ray Meddis, a psychologist at Loughborough University in England. In his book, *The Sleep Instinct*, Dr Meddis, who has been studying sleep for nearly twenty years, agreed that it is tempting to assume that the desire to sleep arises from fatigue. 'In other words the brain knows when it has had a hard day and needs a good rest.' But he thinks we should be suspicious of so simple an answer. 'First, no one has succeeded in showing satisfactorily that physical or mental effort is related to a need for sleep, and, second, observation of people who fly across time zones on long journeys has shown that the brain decides when to be sleepy on the basis of body time – ie the time that it *thinks* it is.'

There is an argument that part of the brain switches on sleep when it thinks the time is right, and that another part switches on wakefulness when the time is right for it, both systems acting independently of the body's muscles and the head's thought processes.

A compatible theory of sleep's function that Dr Meddis and many others have put forward is called the immobilization theory and is based on Darwin's enduring concept that the prime function in the animal world is survival. If you are fish, fowl or fox, the safest time of your day is when you are still and silent, under the cover of darkness, in your rock crevice/roost/den. Here you are least vulnerable to the beast that wants to sink its teeth into you.

Of course, all arguments are just that, and you could say that the giant sloth, which sleeps twenty hours in twenty-four should be proliferating like mad on this basis (assuming that it's not sexually slothful during its waking four) and, conversely, that the Dall porpoise, which, according to those who have studied it, has never been observed to sleep, should be dying out.

It seems unlikely that anyone will convince the mass of humans that their sleep isn't a physical and mental replenishing process, mainly because such theorists have not yet found a homo sapien equivalent to the Dall porpoise. There have been plenty of claims, mind you.

I remember years ago visiting the fine cathedral in the Spanish city of Caceres, south-west of Madrid, little knowing at the time that there was in Caceres a modern marvel far more fascinating to see than any cathedral. It was only later that I learned of the city's Senora Palomino, who claimed that she had not slept for thirty years. One day, while yawning, Senora Palomino had dislocated her jaw, no doubt causing much pain and sleeplessness. The pain eventually went away, but the sleeplessness did not. Thereafter she was said to have remained permanently awake, spending her nights sitting in an armchair, her days running a nursery in her home for about twenty-five children whose mothers worked. That she has not been declared the eighth wonder of the world probably has something to do with her case not being reported by laboratory technicians and eminent scientists but by three hyperbolic British newspapers: the *Sunday People* in 1973, the *Sunday Express* later the same year and *New Reveille* in 1974.

There are, however, many cases of people who throughout long and fruitful lives have mananged on one or two hours sleep. And there are people who, like Senora Palomino, have had their sleep pattern changed suddenly. Dr Dement found a case of this with one of his fellow academics at Stanford University in California. He was Professor B. Morgan, a language scholar, who, until he went to Germany to study at the age of twenty-three, had normally slept up to eight hours. One night he went to bed as usual, at 10 pm, but woke up at 2 am. This four hours a night pattern remained for the rest of his life (he lived into his eighties), and he welcomed it. It enabled him to accomplish more work, and he felt no daytime tired-ness. When he felt like something other than textbooks, Professor Morgan would sit up in bed and knit. His claim to needing only four hours a night was verified in Dr Dement's sleep laboratory. There are also documented examples of people who can get by with even less than

Professor Morgan did, including two Australian men, who required less than three hours a night, and one incredible English woman, who needed only about an hour.

The mechanism that governs our compulsion to shut down the conscious system and let the subconscious trip out of our bodies is rhythmic. Marcel Proust wrote: 'When a man is asleep, he has in a circle around him the chain of the hours, the sequence of the years, the order of the heavenly host.' In a more poetic, more religious age than ours, Proust seemed to grasp what modern researchers have nailed down more plainly: that we, like all matter, dance to a certain rhythm. Night follows day, heat follows cold, storm and calm, wet and dry, tides rise and fall, the moon waxes and wanes. All life is cyclical, full of peaks and troughs, equal and opposite reactions, 'on' and 'off' periods.

In the case of the human body, the particular tune we dance to is called the circadian rhythm, a term coined by a Dr Franz Halberg from the Latin *circa* (about) and *diem* (day) to acknowledge that, like Earth, animals operate on a twenty-four-hour cycle, a biological clock.

The first clue to this hidden rhythm came in 1792 when a man called Jean-Jacques d'Ortous de Mairan played a trick on his heliotrope. The heliotrope plant raises its leaves by day to follow the sun and lowers them at night. The Frenchman put a heliotrope in a dark room for a while and found that it continued to raise its leaves when the sun was up and to lower them when it set, despite being cut off from it. The heliotrope was suffering the equivalent of jetlag.

Jetlag is a good way to illustrate our circadian rhythms, which are often blurred and distorted by the external factors that impinge on our lives – work, play, electric light, alarm clocks, regular meal breaks, monotony, matrimony, and so on. The best evidence of our biological clocks, which, if allowed to find their own level, for most people are set closer to twenty-five hours than twenty-four, is to look at what happens when we cross international time zones. Having to adapt causes circadian dysrhythmia, or jetlag.

Two Australian researchers, Dr Jack Bassett and Dr Robert Spillane, in 1985 published the results of a study of twenty-eight flight attendants on the Sydney-Los Angeles run. They looked at urine samples to examine levels of the hormone cortisol, which rises with emotional and environmental stress, and the attendants kept diaries and filled in questionnaires to record their moods and how they felt physically.

Dr Spillane is an industrial psychologist at the school of management at Sydney's Macquarie University and Dr Bassett, whose PhD is in endocrinology, lectures in the university's school of biological sciences. They studied what happened to the Qantas attendants on two different flights, the first lot having a stopover in Los Angeles of fifty-eight hours and the second having an eighty-two-hour break before returning to Sydney. One would assume that the second lot were the luckier ones. They had many more hours of rest and relaxation before having to fly home again, dispensing coffee, tea, synthetic meals and wide smiles while balancing in a narrow aisle. But this wasn't the case. The flight attendants who had fifty-eight hours' stopover suffered significantly less stress than the others. The eighty-two hour people were kept longer from the natural circadian rhythms that governed their sleep-wake cycles. Their bodies were still on Australian time and trying to regear them to American time was stressful. Bassett and Spillane wrote that the international air traveller's conflict between biological clock and information from the environment is extremely stressful 'and requires an adaptation time in the order of several cycle durations'.

The corollary to the unpleasantness of jetlag is that there is likely to be some benefit from taking care of and reinforcing our circadian rhythms – sticking to the beat. This can be done by developing regular sleep habits. Too much bed can be bad, leading to fragmented, shallow sleep. Getting up at the same time each morning (which, of course, means weekends, too, because circadian rhythms don't take days off) establishes a pattern in the sleep-wake cycle.

Dr Peter Hauri, director of the Dartmouth-Hitchcock Sleep Disorders Center in New Hampshire, USA, says in a guide to sleep disorders he has written for general practitioners: 'Assuming that most humans have an inherent circadian rhythm somewhat longer than twenty-four hours, arising shortly before one is totally "slept out" re-sets the internal clock. If one follows the natural rhythm and sleeps an extra hour, the rhythm will be delayed one hour the first night, two hours the following night, and so on. Sleep onset insomnia may occasionally be the direct result of "sleeping out" each day.'

One of the sleep researchers Dr Hauri mentions in his book is Dr Murray Johns, of Melbourne. Dr Johns says: 'Sleep is like à metronome that sets the tempo and phase of the body rhythms. When is just as important as how long.' Dr Johns, the first Australian to do a PhD on sleep (in 1972), put the metronome theory to the test with a study of the sleep of medical students at Monash University.

Dr Johns was a surgeon at Monash University's Department of Surgery at Melbourne's Alfred Hospital, when, in

1969 he and John Masterton, now associate professor of surgery there, set up the country's first sleep laboratory. They wanted to investigate a theory that the delirium patients often suffer after surgery was related to interference with their rapid eye movement (REM) or dreaming sleep. The theory had arisen because early research by Dr Dement and others in America appeared to indicate that without REM sleep people would eventually go mad. 'The Dement team did not actually say it had linked REM deprivation and psychosis,' says Dr Johns, 'and perhaps it was a case of people reading into things what they want to, but that triggered us off. In fact, what we found in the sleep laboratory was that after, say, major open heart surgery there is *no* REM sleep for a period. One of the lessons we learned in studying sleep after surgery is that medical staff need to help the patients to husband the sleep habit. You have to leave the patient alone to let them recover the habit, not wake them for cleaning, monitoring, etcetera, where it isn't essential. Of course, this is easier to do nowadays because of remote monitoring.'

That experiment triggered Murray Johns's interest in normal people's sleep. He and two colleagues studied 104 fourth-year medical students at Monash University to see if there was a connection between sleep habits and academic performance. They found that poorer academic performance was 'related significantly' to later times of waking up in the morning. Their report on the experiment said: 'Students who performed best at their examinations usually woke up earlier in the morning, both on weekdays and on weekends, and had better quality sleep than students whose academic performance was poorer.' The study showed that at weekends the group with the highest exam marks woke up an average of forty-two minutes earlier than the group with the lowest marks.

They also found that difficulty in falling asleep, awakening during the night, the usual duration of sleep at night or
during the day, and delay before actually getting out of
bed in the morning were all unrelated to academic
performance. As Dr Johns says, the tests on the young
medical students tend to vindicate the adage, 'Early to bed
and early to rise makes a man healthy, wealthy and wise.'

Obviously there are wider implications for the whole
community, particularly for shift workers and for those of
us who fondly believe that we can go out raging on Friday
nights because we can catch up over the weekend.

Biological clocks are as personal as genes. Certainly
many of us (such as the BBC dawn patrol) feel that we
function better if, when allowed, we abandon society's
nine to five, up in the morning, out on the job dictates. I
feel a lot happier, for example, writing this sentence at
10.30 pm. I don't have the restlessness, procrastination
and inability to concentrate that envelops me mid morning. 'Late' people have been shown to reach their
maximum body temperature later in the day than 'early'
folk and to perform less well at set tasks in the morning
than in the afternoon.

What sleep researchers stress about circadian rhythms
is regularity. It's not so much when you go to bed, when
you get up or the amount of time that elapses between the
two that counts, it's the establishment of a pattern of
doing it. An insomniac will scoff at the implication that
sleep is something to turn on and off like a tap, but there
are certain ways to facilitate the flow of sleep, particularly
through sleep 'rituals'.

A further complication of circadian rhythms is that
there are rhythms within rhythms. Humans have not only
a biological day, or circadian rhythm, but also what are
known as biological 'hours', or ultradian rhythms. This

hour is really about ninety or a hundred minutes. When we are awake the ultradian cycle sees us have periods of alertness, efficiency, activity, talking, eating, and so on, followed by a similar period of less concentration and drive – when your get up and go has got up and gone. We're usually too preoccupied with whatever we're doing to be aware of these subtle wheels within the bigger biological wheel, although someone alone and unoccupied in a boring place can be observed to become restless and less restless in ninety to a hundred minute spans. Children in nurseries have been seen to be restless for periods of about thirty-five minutes then quieter and calmer for the next thirty-five, a 'junior' ultradian rhythm of about seventy minutes. Clearly these rhythms within rhythms are important in personal relationships (how often do you realize 'it's not the right moment'?), efficiency at work and our ability to become drowsy before dropping blissfully off to sleep.

Unfortunately, modern life is not organized around such vague concepts as ultradian or circadian rhythms (although Flexitime is a start). So when a person's circadian rhythm is thrown out and he or she is unable to 'free run', sleeping and waking on demand (let's face it, a luxury only for the very rich), he or she usually goes to the local GP and mutters something about 'sleeping trouble'. Often the answer is sleeping pills or anti-depressants, the outcome of which can be to distort further or to disguise the circadian chaos. A more modern approach used by many sleep disorder centres overseas is to shelve the drugs and to set about rewinding the clock. This is called chronotherapy, or time treatment. Take the case of a man who finds that he doesn't fall asleep until 2 am every day. If left alone he would probably get up about 10 am (after eight hours) with no complaint. But having to clock on

earlier means that he's not a happy fellow.
Chronotherapy, which is best done while on holiday or
sick leave for reasons that will become clear, involves the
man holding off going to bed at 2 am, and instead staying
awake until 4. He must get up by noon the next day. On
the second day he must delay sleep a further two hours
until 6 am, getting up by 2 pm the next day. On the third
day he goes to sleep at 8 am and rises at 4 pm, and so on.
Eventually, on the eleventh night, he will be going to bed
at 10 pm and getting up at 6 am. He may modify this to
suit his needs, but he will by this time have reset his
circadian clock.

Chronotherapy isn't necessarily easy; it may require
getting friends or lovers to, as the song says, 'Help Me
Make it Through the Night' while the readjustment is
going on. Taking naps through the day will throw the
reprogramming out, and people with naturally 'weak'
rhythms will remain vulnerable to their body clocks
gaining or losing again if they don't care for them. But it's
not such a daunting thing, particularly in an age when
many people spend vast amounts of time and money
staying fit and eating well when they are awake, and
when sleeping drugs without complications have been
shown to be like free lunches – non-existent.

So we all sleep and wake to a pattern, even though we
don't fully understand why that pattern is imposed. Some
researchers insist that the restoration theory of sleep is
right, citing the fact that growth hormone and muscle-
building substances, such as testosterone, are released
into our blood when we are asleep. They add that,
conversely, the hormones associated with wakefulness,
such as adrenalin and cortiscosteroids, while giving us zip
during the day also hinder the renewal of body tissues.
British psychiatrist Professor Ian Oswald, who runs the

sleep research laboratory at Edinburgh University, Scotland, says: 'Human skin cells renew themselves faster during the time of sleep. The same seems to be true of human blood cells. And we know from studies with animals that every tissue of the body, from the brain to the sole of the foot, renews its structure faster during sleep.'

But the anti-restorationists, such as Ray Meddis, remain unconvinced, suggesting that any repair work the body does could equally happen during times of quiet rest as while awake. That is why Dr Meddis is so keen to find a healthy non-somniac, a certified Senora Palomino. In *The Sleep Instinct* he wrote: 'It is my firm opinion that it will not be long before this occurs. In addition we might hope that, in the not too distant future, physiologists will acquire enough detailed knowledge of sleep control mechanisms for them to be able to disable the system . . . thus producing a totally nonsomniac animal which was otherwise healthy and normal.'

I hope he is wrong. Imagine never seeing the cat curled by the winter hearth, rather staring at you forever with sleepless green eyes. Or worse, picture parents at the end of a long hard day robbed of that ultimate and beautiful command, 'Bedtime!'

TOO MUCH OF A GOOD THING

TOO MUCH sleep is known in the trade as EDS, which stands for excessive daytime sleepiness. The problem also travels under the term 'DOES' or disorders of excessive somnolence. The range extends from heavy midday drowsiness to a condition so severe that its sufferers have been known to fall asleep while copulating.

Excessive daytime sleepiness is not just the penalty of the insomniac; it can happen to people who have a normal night's sleep, although obviously EDS affects those who burn both ends of the candle, either for business or pleasure. And as we have seen, those whose circadian clock is out of kilter and who fall asleep in the late morning are bound for EDS.

Sleep can also be a blanket under which people suffering from depression try to hide, as though unhappiness might be hibernated away like the winter. Manic depressive people, whose moods see-saw, often sleep a lot when 'low' and only little when 'high'. Sufferers from schizophrenia may also fill the void of their withdrawal from the world with sleep. Obviously in these cases excessive sleepiness is a symptom of a bigger problem. But there are many different causes of EDS and in America more people visit sleep disorder centres for DOES than they do for the opposite problem of DIMS or disorders of initiating and maintaining sleep, better known to most as insomnia. This doesn't necessarily mean that daytime sleepiness is more common than night-time lack of it, rather that some types of EDS are life threatening and also because daytime sleepiness is often ill understood and almost frowned upon.

EDS can be caused by something as simple as night-time twitching of the legs. This is a disorder called nocturnal myoclonus and it means that for periods during the night, or perhaps the whole night, one or both of the sufferer's legs will regularly twitch or jerk. Frequently he or she won't even be conscious of it, but the sharp movement causes sleep disturbance, and consequent daytime tiredness. More often than not it is the bed partner who is the real sufferer, and a twitching spouse can lead to separate beds or the divorce court.

The treatment for nocturnal myoclonus is usually administration of a muscle relaxant, although this requires great care. One example of the disorder is provided by a Melbourne man of sixty-five, himself a general practitioner. Dr E explains: 'The problem actually disturbs my wife more than I. When my legs start the violent twitching in the night, I am asleep and quite unaware of the problem. On occasions she gets up and goes to another bed, which she does quite cheerfully and without malice! Sometimes before going off to sleep I am acutely aware of a "restlessness" in my legs, especially my feet, the left one in particular. There is a feeling that the foot is dissociated from the leg, an unpleasant feeling.

'I mentioned this to my own GP, and he thought the problem might be a vascular one associated with the peripheral veins, but I was not convinced.' (Medicos are not the easiest of patients, but by the same token they tend to be either grossly under or over-treated by their colleagues!)' He added that he was prescribed a drug designed to improve blood supply to his limbs, but it was expensive and didn't work.

Nocturnal myoclonus should not be confused with the myoclonic jerks that many people (including the author) get in arms or legs just before dropping off to sleep. These stop once we have been succumbed to sleep whereas if you suffer from nocturnal myoclonus, the legs twitch every twenty or thirty seconds throughout the night.

A more common cause of EDS, one that affects as many as 60,000 Australians, stems from snoring. Not the common or garden sawing noise that is almost like the hum of a motor, but a particular type of snoring that leads to what is called 'sleep apnea syndrome', or failure to breathe while asleep. For these people survival means partially waking perhaps as many as 400 times a night, and therefore feeling totally zonked every day. Apnea sufferers nod off whenever they get the chance – whenever there's a break at work, sitting down at a family barbecue, even driving the car.

The other main cause of serious EDS is the disorder already mentioned called narcolepsy. Unfortunately, like some forms of snoring, it can have fatal consequences. To make matters worse, many doctors know nothing about it. The American Narcolepsy Association estimates that there are 250,000 sufferers in the US, although only about one-third of them have been diagnosed, that is, about 165,000 Americans lead grim lives because of narcolepsy but are frequently dismissed as malingerers. The Narcolepsy Association says: 'Typically a person who is diagnosed as suffering from narcolepsy has lived with the symptoms for ten to fifteen years and has sought help from three to five doctors before correct diagnosis.' If American and British estimates are right, there are probably 17,000 narcoleptics in Australia, although the majority of them won't know it.

It is hard to think of a disorder more cruel than narcolepsy. It is a condition of hypersomnolence, which means almost permanent sleepiness. A narcoleptic is sleepy, even when he or she has had a good eight-hour sleep every night. Apart from living life in a permanent state of sleep-fog, there are three other symptoms: cataplexy, sleep paralysis and hallucinations.

Cataplexy is a state Edgar Allan Poe may have unwittingly observed before he wrote *The Premature Burial*. The victim may fall down as though stricken by a bolt from the blue, so much so that he or she may appear to be dead. The cause of this collapse is an instant loss of muscle tone. What appears to happen is a sudden, inappropriate onset of REM or dream sleep. REM sleep is also known as paradoxical sleep because, while the eyes move under their lids and the mind is actively dreaming, the body is virtually paralysed, our limbs are completely limp; only those muscles necessary for the eyeballs to move and for breathing are working.

For most of us this is not a problem; we go to sleep gradually in our bed or chair in front of the television, and even then our first period of paralysed REM sleep doesn't usually begin until between seventy and ninety minutes after sleep onset. But the narcoleptic suffering a bout of cataplexy plunges straight from being awake into this muscle-less sleep. There are degrees of seriousness. An attack may be fleeting, lasting only a few seconds. In some people the attack may affect only the upper part of the body so that the head, shoulders and arms sag. In others there will be full collapse for several minutes after which the victim has to pick up the pieces of a grossly interrupted life. In the worst cases a sufferer can fall to the

ground asleep mid stride. The boss may be delivering a
sermon on the monthly sales figures and the narcoleptic
will fall asleep in the middle of it; a group of friends may
be at a restaurant and the narcoleptic will plunge head-
first into the vichyssoise; a narcoleptic car driver may
depart the road for a broad-girthed tree. An attack of
cataplexy may hit at the most crucial moment of lovemaking, turning an ecstatic orgasm into an excruciatingly
embarrassing snorgasm. The reason for this is that one of
the main trigger mechanisms of cataplexy is strong
emotion. Laughter and anger are almost guaranteed to
send the sufferer into slumped sleep.

It seems hard to believe that emotion and excitement
can have such unlikely consequences, but one Australian
researcher has seen it with her own eyes under hospital
conditions. Kathleen Phillips is a registered polysomnographics technician, or sleep recorder, the only one in this
country. She works in the sleep laboratory at the Royal
Prince Alfred Hospital in Sydney. Kathleen Phillips
learned her skills at the sleep unit run by Dr Dement at
Stanford University and while there met some sufferers of
cataplexy. 'One man we just told jokes to, and he would
be gone,' she says. 'We had to record this on film and an
electroencephalogram (which measures brain activity) to
convince some neurologists that he was not having fits.'
Cataplexy has a strong genetic component and, although
doctors don't know what causes narcolepsy, it appears to
have physiological rather than psychological roots. A
study of narcoleptic dogs showed that, when bred selec-
tively, they pass the disorder on to their pups: 'There were
some dobermans and poodles at Stanford that would drop
to the ground asleep as soon as you got them excited,'
recalls Kathleen Phillips.

This devastating onset of sleep can have horrific as well

as hilarious consequences. More than 40 per cent of the people in America eventually diagnosed as having narcolepsy report that they have been involved in car accidents. Socially, their lives can be miserable. Spouses and offspring will see them as uninterested and rude. Take, for example, Vincent Smith, a retired builder of Basin View, near Nowra in New South Wales. Until he was diagnosed as a narcolepic at the Royal Prince Alfred unit in Sydney, all he knew was that for most of his life he had been sleepy. Now in his sixties, Vince Smith first became aware that he had a problem when he was about twenty-five and he fell asleep while standing up in a train. Miraculously he managed to survive as a builder, probably because he was able to predict the onset of an episode, which is something not all narcoleptics can do. (In America, the car accident rate of diagnosed narcolpetics is *lower* than that of normal drivers, presumably because those who continue to drive after diagnosis have the ability to pull off the road before an attack. In some US states, doctors are required to report narcolepsy sufferers to driving licence authorities.)

'In the end,' says Vince Smith, 'I did have to give up work. I was scared that I would fall off a building.' It was his second wife, Joy, who helped him discover that he suffered from narcolepsy. 'I felt like murdering him at times,' she says. 'I thought I was so boring because he would go to sleep in the middle of me saying something. In the end, his seeking help was a condition of us getting married.' Vince Smith's problem was shown graphically on the ABC programme, 'Open File', in April 1985, when he fell asleep in the middle of an interview about it. After a few minutes he woke, blinked a bit then tried to resume the conversation.

Retired, spending most of his time at home and with a well-informed and understanding wife, Vince Smith can cope. But imagine how hard narcolepsy can be for a child or student. Although there is no clear pattern, narcolepsy most often first appears between the ages of fifteen and twenty. Someone regularly falling asleep in the classroom is likely to be accused of too much television watching, laziness, drugtaking or plain inability to learn.

EDS and cataplexy are the biggest crosses the narcoleptic must bear. Another frequent symptom is sleep paralysis, something that can also be found in people who are not narcoleptic. This is the feeling of paralysis some people get just before falling asleep or just after waking; it can last a few seconds or several agonizing minutes. Sufferers can blink and move their eyes, but no more, and it can be accompanied by vivid hallucinations, known either as hypnagogic (before sleep) or hypnopompic (after sleep).

'Jim A', a twenty-five-year-old Greek musician who lives with his family in the Melbourne suburb of Camberwell, says: 'I've had this condition now for about six years and have been to doctors, a clinic and tried meditation.' He does suffer from daytime sleepiness, but not excessively, and he says he doesn't have attacks of cataplexy, so he's probably not a narcoleptic. He does, however, know all about sleep paralysis and hallucination.

'It's hard to describe,' he says, 'because in this state I'm mentally aware and as though I'm relaxing with my eyes closed. I can actually open my eyes and see the room, but my whole body is paralysed. I can feel the sheets above and below me and the position I'm in at that time. It is a frightening experience because in this state I have "supernatural vizualization". A few times I have felt that my whole awareness has moved from my eyes to my heart, and that I can actually feel the blood moving in and out of it.'

His paralysis and hallucination appear to be hypno-pompic, or after he has slept. 'I get into a state of paralysis through a dream or thought,' he says. 'I think to myself, Oh, no, not again, and sometimes repeat to myself the mantra I learned in meditation, which usually takes away a bit of the fear. Different things happen . . . sometimes I feel that my soul has moved out of my body to different areas of my room, or I can see little creatures next to my bed, or see my brother or mother. Sometimes the paralysis is so strong I begin to scream for help. The only way I have been able to get out of this paralysis is to try to move my body, my arms, head and legs, from side to side. This might last fifteen to twenty seconds before I break out of the state. The moving is a tremendous strain on my body, and my heart rate increases unbelievably, ready to jump out of my body.'

'Jim A' is a rather lonely man and admits that his father thinks he's a 'no-hoper'. He sleeps eight to eight and a half hours a night, has a well-ordered work-play-eat routine and says that his physical and mental state has been improved by meditation. 'It has given me greater inner strength (for example, to stop taking sleep pills) and more direction in life, but my sleep paralysis still occurs. People have suggested that I remain in the paralysed state and just relax as it will go away on its own. I'm afraid of doing this as I feel that I might never wake up.'

Such frightening paralysis and hallucination tend to be more common just before rather than just after sleep, but in both cases they represent, as with cataplexy, something normal happening at an abnormal time; that is, the paralysis and imaginative flights that we have normally during sleep are happening in wakefulness.

There is no magic tablet to take for narcolepsy, although that doesn't mean that the estimated 17,000 Australians who have some form of it are better left undiagnosed. (One US estimate puts the incidence of narcolepsy at four per 10,000, equally spread among males and females. This lower figure would mean that about 6,500 Australians suffer from narcolepsy.) The worst effects of EDS and cataplexy can be ameliorated, the former by careful use of stimulants such as amphetamines (narcoleptics tend to become alert rather than high on speed), the latter by using tricyclic anti-depressant drugs. These ubiquitous drugs (they are also used for bedwetting) may work through suppressing the onset of REM sleep. But tricyclic anti-depressants have strings, among them dryness of the mouth, blurred vision, and the last thing a person with EDS wants, drowsiness. The Catch 22 is that tricyclic anti-depressants can also cause impotence, thus a narcoleptic may suffer an attack of cataplexy if he has sex, but may not be able to try if he takes the tablets.

One help to narcoleptics is frequent daytime napping. A regular five or ten-minute zizz seems to forestall the unexpected collapse. Certainly this seems to help in the case of Vincent Smith. Even tiny 'micro-sleeps' of a few seconds' duration may work. Salvador Dali is reported to have a suitably surreal method of napping. He's said to sit in a chair, his arm on a rest and a spoon in his hand. On the floor below is an enamel plate. When he falls asleep the spoon drops, hits the plate and wakes him. In the interval of its falling Dali is said to claim complete refreshment.

Bizarre though that may sound, Dr William Orr, director of the sleep disorders centre at Presbyterian Hospital, Oklahoma, reports the case of someone about as different from Dali as you could get – a fifty-two-year-old US army officer – using a similar trick to handle sudden sleep onset. The man is described as falling asleep

inappropriately, particularly when eating, driving or having sex. Although such attacks are usually beyond the
narcoleptic's power to fight, this man had a way of
dealing with his embarrassing habit of falling asleep while
being addressed by his superiors. He held a set of keys in
his hand and when he fell asleep the noise of them hitting
the floor would wake him.

The army officer's problems steadily worsened, however, and he had his first episode of cataplexy while out
fishing with his daughter. He caught a fish, which made
him excited, which made him collapse and fall in the lake.
Eventually he would have two or three such episodes a
day, and he also suffered sleep paralysis and pre-sleep
hallucinations. The problem was eventually diagnosed
and his family and superior officers were told. The latter,
presumably figuring that he was not the ideal soldier for
the firing line, assigned him to non-hazardous duties and
allowed him to schedule two twenty-minute naps a day.

Apart from narcolepsy and excessive sleepiness caused
by disorders such as nocturnal leg twitching and the lethal
snoring syndrome called apnea, there is another affliction
where people suffer from too much of a good thing. It is
called idiopathic CNS hypersomnolence, idiopathic
meaning of unknown origin. The sufferer can fight off
sleep if he or she must but will sleep for hours and hours if
left to his or her own devices – from twelve to twenty in a
day. The hypersomniac will sleep through the alarm and
keep on going, and even then will arise groggy and fuzzy,
so much so that he or she will appear to be almost drunk.

As with most things in life, the sheets are always softer
on the other side. Hypersomnolence is the stuff
insomniacs dream of – or it would be if only they could get
off to sleep.

TOO LITTLE
OF A GOOD THING

INSOMNIA probably nudges the cold into second place as the world's most common complaint. It's about as hard to define as the cold, and as difficult to treat. Just as the cold has fostered wonder 'solutions', ranging from putting garlic in your shoes to gobbling vitamin C, so insomniacs have long sought the cure. Louis XIV reckoned the secret was always to have the right bed for your mood and to make sure that cool sheets and pillows were available (it seems strange that the Sun King hated a hot bed), for which reasons he is said to have had 413 beds at Versailles. Another anti-hot-sheet man was Benjamin Franklin, who, in a less grandiose way than Louis XIV, rotated between the four beds he kept in his room, the only drawback being that his wife had difficulty tracking him down in the dark.

The system Socrates used was to get up and think away his insomnia. Again, as many sufferers find with this method, there are frequently drawbacks for spouses. His wife is alleged to have emptied the chamber pot from beneath their bed on to the head of Socrates as he paced the courtyard below. Perhaps this provides the derivation of the stirring phrase, 'Sock it to him.'

The biggest problem in discussing insomnia is that if nobody knows exactly why we sleep or how much of it is

necessary, how can you know if you are not getting
enough? We have seen that hypersomnolents can consume two-thirds of their lives abed, but what about the
other end of the spectrum, those who can almost do
without sleep? Two clues to sleep need come from
deprivation tests and from case studies of people, who, if
not quite like the legendary Senora Palomino, can be
called healthy insomniacs.

In April 1985, a more modern Greek than Socrates
displayed a remarkable ability to do without sleep while
under great physical stress. Yiannis Kouros, a twenty-
nine-year-old caretaker, ran the Sydney-Melbourne mar-
athon in the record time of five days, five hours, seven
minutes and fifty-four seconds. Yiannis Kouros chopped
more than nine hours from the time set by elderly potato
farmer Cliff Young, despite the course, at 960 kilometres,
being 90 kilometres longer than when Young won in
1983. Everyone, especially Melbourne's huge Greek community, sang Yiannis Kouros's praises for this stunning
feat of endurance, accomplished on a diet of Greek cakes,
chocolate and fruit.

What got scant attention was the fact that he had slept
only seven and a half hours during the 125 that elapsed
from start to finish. Yiannis Kouros's coach, Takis
Skoulos, said his runner had remained mentally alert
throughout the race, adding that at one stage Kouros had
become angry because he'd wanted twenty minutes sleep
and had been allowed half an hour. Kouros said at the
finish that he thought it would take a week for him to
'catch up' on his sleep. It seemed a secondary problem; he
said it would take a month for his feet to recover.

A more remarkable case of deprivation is that of Randy
Gardner, who, in a US high school science fair in 1965,
challenged the then world record for going without sleep

– 260 hours. Sleep researcher William Dement read about the attempt in a newspaper and took the opportunity to monitor it. Eighty hours had elapsed by the time Dr Dement and a colleague from Stanford University, Dr George Gulevitch, met Randy Gardner, but his schoolmates attested that he had not slept up to that point. The watchers found that as more time passed it required increasing efforts by them to keep him awake and motivated during the long nights; by day it was relatively easy. One successful device was for Dr Dement and Randy Gardner to play hundreds of games on pinball machines (all of which Gardner won).

Finally, before dozens of TV cameras and press reporters, Randy Gardner said goodnight at 6.12 am, not having slept for 264 hours and 12 minutes. 'It's just mind over matter,' said the very fit seventeen-year-old before sliding gratefully between sheets. Only fourteen hours and forty minutes later, he awoke again, feeling good. He stayed awake for about twenty-four hours, then slept for eight. In no time his sleep pattern was normal, and he showed no signs of any ill effects.

The experiment helped to show that sleep deprivation would not automatically lead to madness, as many had believed, and some still do. Randy Gardner did have one or two minor hallucinatory experiences during the attempt, but he showed no paranoid or psychotic behaviour.

You can always find contradictions, of course, and certainly many of us do behave oddly when kept too long from our beds. Six years before Randy Gardner's record, a New York DJ called Peter Tripp sat in a glass booth in Times Square and stayed awake for 200 hours in a fundraising effort. Eventually his speech began to slur and towards the very end he showed acute paranoid psychosis at night, convinced that people were trying to drug his food and drink to send him to sleep. It may be argued that disc jockeys have a propensity for paranoia (or for driving others to it!), but when he was a medical student, Dr Dement admitted to feelings of ridiculous suspicion about his fellow students after depriving himself of sleep for only forty-eight hours.

The point is that people like Yiannis Kouros and Randy Gardner show that peak functioning without the regulation eight hours' sleep is not impossible, a fact that can lead to the conclusion widely held among sleep researchers that insomnia is often self-fulfilling through unnecessary worry and that many insomniacs would do better to throw off the label as they throw off the blankets and embrace the fact that they are short sleepers. (I find that sentences as long as the one you have just read – 72 words – are an excellent cure for insomnia, and one easily found in newspaper editorials, so instead of lying there counting sheep, see how long you can spin out a sentence, the basic rule being that everything but a full stop is allowed and that it's cheating to whack in an 'and' between any old random clauses – see what I mean, this parenthetical pill is already eighty words long, and . . .).

Although insomnia is not really to be dismissed so flippantly, it is worth looking at some examples of happy short sleepers.

In 1967, just two years after Randy Gardner's effort, a young Australian doctor called Henry Jones and a visiting Scot called Ian Oswald found, through a Perth newspaper, several people who claimed to sleep very little. (Today Dr Jones is executive director of health services for Western Australia and Professor Oswald runs the sleep laboratory at Edinburgh University and is a world authority on the subject.) Among those the two doctors interviewed were two men who said they slept only about three hours a night and had no complaints about it.

The men, only one of whom is still alive, said they were short sleepers mainly because they led very full lives. At the time 'Harry M' was fifty-four and said that for at least twenty years he had slept only three hours a night. Put another way, during that time he had been awake a bit over four years more than a 'normal' eight-hours a day sleeper. His wife, a professional woman, confirmed 'Harry M's' story, and he spent seven nights having his sleep studied by doctors Jones and Oswald, during which time he averaged two hours and forty-seven minutes a night. He did say that sometimes at weekends he would take a nap in the daytime, although usually only for a few minutes. The doctors described him as looking his true age of fifty-four and as giving an impression of vigour and restlessness.

The second man, 'John H', was then a thirty-year-old draughtsman, and on six nights of readings he averaged two hours and forty-three minutes' sleep. His wife also confirmed that this was habitual. 'John H' explained that about six years earlier he had decided to reduce the time he spent sleeping because he was so busy. He added that his father had done the same when he was younger and often had not gone to bed at all at nights. 'John H' did say that he would sleep a bit longer if he took holidays, but he hadn't had one for some years. Apart from his work, he was secretary to several church and youth organizations and he would do their paper work during the long nights. The doctors also noted that he looked no more haggard than the normal thirty-year-old and described him as a 'vigorous and over-meticulous' man.

By monitoring the two men's brain activity using an electroencephalogram, it was revealed that they appeared to have unusual stages of sleep. As we have seen there are two types of sleep: REM (rapid eye movement) and non-REM (non-rapid eye movement). Within non-REM there are three or four stages. The first is that not unpleasant borderline between full wakefulness and sleep, usually lasting from half a minute to seven minutes. Stage 2 non-REM sleep is bona fide sleep and can be confirmed on the printout from an electroencephalogram machine by tight bunches of lines known as spindles. Stage 3 is called delta sleep, deeper still (some experts like to refer to a fourth stage, an even deeper level of delta sleep). During the night the stages come and go gradually in cycles, with the first burst of REM – and dreaming – coming between seventy and ninety minutes after sleep onset. The REM periods get longer as the night wears on. Everybody has REM sleep. The people who are adamant that they don't dream are mistaken; it's just that most of us don't recall having dreamt if we awaken during a non-REM stage of sleep.

With the truncated sleep of 'Harry M' and 'John H' there appeared to be what the doctors referred to as a 'pressure' for more REM sleep than is usually found in a normal person's first three hours. This appeared to be at the expense of stage 2 sleep. Dr Jones and Dr Oswald contrasted their results with those of an experiment in which eight volunteers were restricted to only three hours sleep a night for eight nights. With these people, an average of only 7.5 per cent of their three hours was spent in REM sleep, while 'Harry M' and 'John H' averaged 23.5 per cent REM sleep in the same time. This does not prove anything, but perhaps 'Harry M' and 'John H' were twice blessed, they could cope very well with only a bit more than a third of the sleep most people 'need', and they still got their fair share of dreams.

A more remarkable case than that of these two Australians has been documented by Dr Ray Meddis, the man who has raised many questions about why we sleep and who says there are holes in the traditional argument that sleep is for physical restoration. Although Dr Meddis has not yet discovered a total non-sleeper, in 1973 he found a seventy-year-old retired nurse who said she slept for only an hour a night, with no daytime naps. Dr Meddis and two colleagues at Bedford College, London University, reported their findings as 'An Extreme Case of Healthy Insomnia' in the journal *Electroencephalography and Clinical Neurophysiology.*

The doctors interviewed 'Mary M', who although retired kept herself busy with writing and painting. She told them she despised inactivity, but they found no evidence of hypomania, or manic behaviour. Before she came into the laboratory, 'Mary M' was asked to record her sleep for a fortnight, and the sleep log she presented showed an average sleep time of forty-nine minutes in twenty-four hours.

'Mary M' was happy to be tested in the laboratory, but she pointed out that such novel surroundings might make her feel even more awake than usual. So Dr Meddis and his colleagues made two separate investigations. In the first one, over three days, 'Mary M', as she had predicted, didn't sleep at all for the first two days and had a total of twenty-nine minutes on the third. In the second study, over five successive days, she averaged sixty-seven minutes' sleep a night, without any signs of sleep deprivation. The doctors reported that at no time did 'Mary M' ever complain of drowsiness or lack of sleep, and she appeared to feel sorry for people who 'wasted so much time' sleeping. She did say that she would become tired physically, when she would sit down to rest her legs, but she said she never felt sleepy. At nights she would sit on her bed (she didn't lie down) and pass the time reading, painting, writing or crocheting. As a rule she would fall asleep about 2 am, waking fully refreshed about 3 am.

Dr Meddis and his colleagues said they were at a loss to explain why 'Mary M' slept so little, but added that her case seemed to be incompatible with the theory that substantial amounts of sleep are needed for the recovery of mind and body. They noted the studies by Doctor Jones and Doctor Oswald and said that, unlike the two Australian men, 'Mary M' did not show increased REM sleep, hers, if anything, being slightly less than normal. Dr Meddis made a point of not calling 'Mary M' an insomniac on the basis that she did not have trouble falling or remaining asleep and that she had no complaint about her condition.

One professed non-somniac I have met is 'Bill W', a voluble, articulate man who is also a snorer.

Bill is what you could call a builder/wrecker; he's very talented with his hands, but he drinks too much. He says: 'I only need two or three hours sleep a night, with possibly a twenty to thirty-minute sleep during the daytime, unless I have been drinking heavily, when I will sleep six or seven hours. As is the case with most excessive drinkers, I have gone up to five days with no sleep at all while recovering from a "bender", with no serious effects.' He adds an aside that, as a drunk, he has observed another quirk of sleep after alcohol – the loss of sense of direction when aroused. 'I have shared premises at various times with people who, upon wanting to relieve themselves in the middle of the night, sleepwalk to the hall cupboard, wardrobe or pantry and urinate over everything. This, thankfully, has not happened to me, but the habit is very common and keeps many wives awake after social functions, ready to steer their spouses out of doors.'

Somehow I don't think 'Bill W' and the sprightly 'Mary M' would have had much to share as non-somniacs. But I suspect Bill's right about nocturnal disorientation, even without the blurring effects of booze. I remember my own son's example many years ago in London when he was about four. One day we rearranged his bedroom, which was right next to the bathroom. He got up in the middle of the night and took the few steps that habit told him led to the lavatory, forgetting the day's arrangements. We awoke to find him contentedly peeing on a lamp we'd put on a low table in one corner of the room.

None of this will be of any comfort to someone who just can't get off to sleep or who does so only to awake and remain that way until the first bird heralds another hard day. Insomnia is known in sleep medicine terminology as DIMS – disorders of initiating and maintaining sleep.

It is also probably of little reassurance to the insomniac to learn that long sleepers (people who habitually sleep more than nine hours) tend to be worriers and non-conformists, scoring lower than short sleepers on tests for sociability, tolerance and flexibility. Short sleepers (people who sleep less than six hours) tend to be energetic, outgoing and ambitious. What helps even less is the fact that insomnia is often frowned upon, those who suffer it frequently being labelled neurotic or depressive for lying there pining like Macbeth:

> Sleep that knits up the ravell'd sleeve of care,
> The death of each day's life, sore labour's bath,
> Balm of hurt minds, great nature's second course,
> Chief nourisher in life's feast.

The causes of insomnia can be of mind, body or environment. It worsens as we grow older, and it is more common
among women than men. It has been estimated that 15
per cent of patients attending their family GP complain of
insomnia and that, in middle age, a quarter of all women
take drugs or non-prescription recipes to help them sleep.

The most obvious cause of sleeplessness is a big worry,
leading to what the Americans call 'transient or situa-
tional insomnia'. We've all had emotional upsets – falling
in love or crashing back out of it, for example – that have
kept us awake, so much so that resort is made to the bottle
of hypnotic drugs to break the pattern.

Answers to these problems rarely come out of a bottle,
however, and chronic use of hypnotics may impair sleep,
reduce waking performance, and mask underlying medical or psychological problems. Obviously there are differences between insomnia caused by short-term depression
triggered by circumstance and that caused by deep-seated
and enduring endogenous depression. Strangely it has
been found that one of the best treatments for people with
serious depression is to deprive them of sleep. An
experiment in 1975 showed that endogenously depressed
patients were helped greatly when they were awakened
from most of their REM sleep. The value of such
therapeutic deprivation is that it can be used to bridge the
gap of two or three weeks before anti-depressant drugs
become effective.

Environmental causes of insomnia are more obvious. If
you are too hot, too cold, too hungry, overfed, sleeping on
a bed of nails or in the flight path of Concorde, you are
less likely to find the 'chief nourisher' closing your
eyelids. An ideal temperature for humans to sleep at has
not yet been found, although it is known that we have

more disturbed sleep when the mercury is above 24°C. At the other extreme, arctic conditions of 5°C and below have been shown to have a sharp affect on REM sleep, cutting it by about 25 per cent.

People who lose weight usually have sleep reductions and, conversely, weight gain is associated with longer sleep. It can be seen that there is something Darwinian in this: a hungry animal won't be sleeping, it will be out looking for a meal, while a sated fat cat will be curled up having a good kip.

Noise, too, is an obvious cost to sleep. A study of people living near the Los Angeles airport showed that they averaged forty-five minutes less sleep each night than did a similar number of people in a quieter part of the city of angels. In London, 6,000 people living near Heathrow were interviewed about aircraft noise, and a disproportionate number of them had problems of getting to sleep and of waking during the night. The greatest difficulty was experienced by those who felt angry about the planes rather than those who regarded the noise as an annoying fact of life, the message being that emotional reaction to noise may be as significant as the decibels. Constant predictable noise, such as an airconditioner, is more easily adjusted to than is random intrusion, such as a plane, police siren or workers using a jackhammer on the road outside. Some people can even become noise dependent for their sleep, as in the tale of the miller who couldn't drop off without the sound of his big stones grinding the wheat.

If you take the environ out of environmental, you get another cause of insomnia – mental activity, and the problem of how to stop it. The common answer is to divert the fretful mind to other things in the hope that sleep will surreptitiously seduce you while you're not watching. One such recipe for this was sent to me by a Melbourne woman. She wrote:

'My rendition, besides relaxation, includes the basic fact of acceptance of the condition and using the time normally spent worrying to:

1 Read the book that appeals to you.

2 Watch the amazing brainwashing techniques used in early morning cartoons on TV for children, such as Mr Magoo, Leonardo the King, etc.

3 Write thank you and other letters.

4 Have a honey and whisky drink.

5 Physical exercise and relaxation of muscles one by one.

6 Play or listen to your favourite piece of music. Baroque music is very suitable. Vivaldi, Handel and Purcell are all good. Don't choose spicy, dramatic pieces with a lot of changing dynamics and prima donnas telling you they've killed their mothers, all in Italian. Choose something rhythmically pleasant and clockwork. Mozart's good, too – 'Eine Kleine Nachtmusik.'

7 Review the things which are swirling around in your mind. List them in any order as they come to you. Can you solve any of them? Can you act on them or assist a solution now? Some examples of temporary solutions which may assist a real solution and help you to pacify your mind: write a letter to the person you had an argument with and post it in the morning. Ring a radio station, start by answering a relevant question, then persuade them to talk about your problem! This may lead to an insomniacs' hour with relaxation techniques over the radio – say 2 am!

8 Serapax, Valium, Mogadon (avoid this one).

9 Ask yourself these questions: have I got a regular get-up habit in the morning? Have I got a place to sleep which

does not include any other activity? (Sleeping is more important than sex. You can't survive without sleep, so you may have to sleep in a separate bed or another room.) How much exercise do I do during the day, the week? Can I solve some of the matters that persist in tumbling over and over in my head by worrying about them?'

More suggestions can be found in chapter seven, but the woman's nine commandments are probably as good as most experts' offerings. Few of them would quibble with any but the fourth, the one recommending a whisky and honey. Modern sleep studies have ruled out the nightcap and the hot toddy. Although it is true that alcohol makes many people sleep, it is also a leading cause of bad sleep. Sleep quality is as important as quantity. Alcohol, although it might appear to ease the insomniac's burden through its undoubted ability to lower anxiety, fragments the sleep that follows and typically reduces the total amount of time slept. In the end, nightcaps may cause rather than cure poor sleep.

Certainly most experts would support the main thrust of the list, which is that the insomniac has to rein in the terrible fears that usually go with sleeplessness, so that the worry feeds the insomnia in a vicious circle. One man who is helping a lot of people to break out of this self-defeating routine in Michael Young, a psychologist at the University of New South Wales, in Sydney. He puts insomniacs into two broad types, after any biological cause has been ruled out. He says there are people with a very long history of insomnia, often going back to childhood, who have a natural tendency to be easily triggered emotionally. The second lot are those who do not have a highly labile, or unstable, nervous system but whose way of life and tendency to worry, or both, cause high levels of arousal.

Michael Young runs clinics for insomniacs using mainly relaxation therapy, what psychologists call 'the behavioural aspirin'. He says he finds that often just talking to people, explaining insomnia, reassuring them that they are not alone and educating them about reasonable sleep expectations and individual requirements helps them greatly.

Although he is keen on relaxation therapy, Michael Young is aware that classes involve quite a lot of time and effort, and he is sceptical about relaxation tapes that people are meant to listen to at home. 'The problem with them,' he says, 'is that people won't comply with what's needed and keep up the work. In one experiment, people were given tapes with a fifteen-minute relaxation programme. Unknown to them, a device sealed inside the recorders they were given registered how often and for how long it was used. A month later they were collected on the pretence of repairs, and the devices showed that while 75 per cent of the people *said* they were following the programme, only 25 per cent were. My guess is that after three months only 10 per cent of the people would be sticking to it.'

Young's research led him to look into auditory stimulation and the effects of noise on sleep. 'As you go deeper into the later stages of sleep, it is interesting that the wave patterns shown on the electroencephalogram machine become more regular, hence its sometimes being referred to as "S sleep", for synchronized,' he says. 'So what would be the effect of continuous waves of white noise (white noise being meaningless sound requiring no interpretation)? People have tried various noises and chimes at various intervals. We know that a monotone doesn't help; it has to be something with a cadence, a rise and fall.'

After lots of testing Young opted for a shhhhhhhhh

noise, something a bit like the sound of distant surf. The consensus was that this was the most pleasant; people didn't mind leaving it on. He played the sound on a machine during our interview in his office at the university. It was not at all intrusive. But it's not really like surf because the sound is constant, and never varies. Anyone living near a surf beach, as I do, knows that real wave noise can actually keep you awake as you listen for the different cracks, roars, hisses and rumbles up the shore.

Michael Young got one of the university's electrical departments to make up a device using this surf sound about the size of Freud's 871-page opus, *The Interpretation of Dreams*. He calls the thing a 'surf sound sleep inducer' and has about sixty of them on trial with insomniacs (they pay only for the parts, about $60). Young says: 'In trials, so far, the surf sound sleep inducer has had equivalent results to those we get from rigorously applied relaxation methods, with the obvious advantage of requiring less time from therapist and patient.'

Early results indicated that the machine does more to keep people asleep than to send them off. Some of the users have said, 'It's a hook to hang my thoughts on', or, 'It attracts my thoughts like a magnet.' Young has a lot of sympathy for insomniacs and is critical of many doctors' attitudes to them. 'It really gets up my nose that many of them are treated as neurotic depressives,' he says. 'They are not significantly more depressed, and they don't necessarily worry more than others. If they are slightly depressed, it may be because they have good cause to be – they have a sleep problem. One woman said to me, "Please don't call me that (*insomniac*), it makes me feel that I'm considered crazy." This was an impression she had got after visiting her GP.'

Michael Young's research also makes use of a device

called a sleep monitor, which was invented by another
member of the University of New South Wales, Emeritus
Professor Syd Lovibond. It is an effective, low-cost way of
measuring how much time a person sleeps, and it is far
less invasive than an electroencephalograph machine,
which requires electrodes to be attached to the patient's
head. It won't tell you about the quality of sleep, the way
an electroencephalograph reveals the time spent dreaming and not dreaming, but it can show quantity. The
monitor emits a regular chiming sound. Each time it
chimes, the user presses a button to record that he or she
has heard it and, therefore, is awake. When the person
drops off, the button is no longer pressed, and the time
awake and asleep is recorded. The sleep monitor can also
measure how often and for how long the surf sound sleep
inducer is used. Michael Young mentions that those who
have dropped out of his trials (only about 5 per cent)
usually have done so not because they dislike the surf
sound but because their partner claims to. He suspects this
may say more about the relationship than the invasive-
ness of the noise.

Like many other sleep researchers, Michael Young has
come to realize that insomnia is often the triumph of
expectation over need. This can be particularly so with
older people, poor and disrupted sleep becoming more
frequent with age. Many old people seek to compensate
for 'poor nights' with daytime naps, or resort to medication. Michael Young and Joy Rae, a Sydney nurse who is
also a psychologist, put the expectation against need
theory to the test with a group of people aged between
sixty and eighty-five at a community centre in the Sydney
suburb of Maroubra. First, Michael Young spoke to them
on sleep and insomnia and then involved them in a
programme of relaxation techniques. At the same time all

of the elderly citizens were taken off their regular sleep-inducing medication. Two months later they were reassessed. The result was that while they were not necessarily sleeping better or longer, most of them had given up or greatly reduced their medication. Michael Young says: 'This was significant for them personally and, of course, it indicates enormous potential savings for the economy in drug costs.'

Apart from conditioned over-expectation of sleep, some insomniacs suffer what is called 'conditioned wakefulness', or poor conditioning. What this boils down to is that the symbols most people readily associate with sleep – bedroom, bed, mattress, sheets, pillows, even doing your teeth – can act for some as triggers for arousal. This is another aspect of the self-fulfilling nature of some insomnia: the very things that should help us to sleep, such as softness, darkness and warmth, instead bring on frustration, tension and stress, all of which act to keep us awake. Often the answer can be to desert the bedroom, to try another room, or the floor. Sometimes this conditioned wakefulness will mean that someone complaining of insomnia will sleep very well in a sleep laboratory, it being so different from the symbols at home that over a long period have become associated with denied sleep.

Maladaptive conditioning can happen to babies, too, although you have to be careful here not to confuse it with manipulative conditioning, where the baby wraps Mum and Dad around its little finger. Babies don't suffer insomnia; they take what they need, which is often about fourteen hours out of twenty-four in the first few weeks of life, reducing to ten or twelve hours a day after a year or two. Like the rest of us, however, there is no firm line; some babes are short sleepers, some long. Most youngsters do settle into a reasonably acceptable sleep routine (for their parents) by the time they are four. It is all part of life's rich tapestry that when they're about fourteen and lurching into adolescence it is bloody nigh impossible to get them *out* of their beds, especially for school on Mondays.

One approach to insomnia caused by poor conditioning has been put to the test by a Melbourne man, Dr David Morawetz. He is not a medico (his doctorate is in economics), but David Morawetz decided to add a master's degree in psychology to his qualifications and chose for his thesis an evaluation of a self-help, non-drug treatment for insomnia. He got about 150 poor sleepers in Melbourne to try a programme based on a tape commercially available in the United States.

'It's not something you play when you go to bed,' David Morawetz explains. 'It first helps you to diagnose what your sleep problem is, then it helps you to work out what to do to solve it. It tries an eclectic approach, using some relaxation therapy. But that's not central to it. It's what's called a stimulus control treatment. The essence is that some people start to sleep badly for some good reason, like an enormous amount of stress, somebody dying, a car accident, God knows what, and they get into the habit of sleeping badly. The idea is to try to break the habit. For instance, bed often becomes associated with 'not-sleep'; the person can sleep in front of the TV or on a couch, or wherever they are, but not when they go to bed. They think they are not going to be able to fall asleep, so they can't. Bed becomes a place where you eat, watch TV, read, do anything other than sleep. So the aim is to reverse all that, to associate bed with sleep and sleep with bed, no sleeping when you are not in bed, no sleeping during the day, no eating, reading, watching TV or anything else in bed.

'In particular, if you go to bed and find that you are not asleep within ten or fifteen minutes, you get up, go to another room, do something you enjoy and then, when you are ready to go back to sleep, you go back to bed. If you are not asleep within ten or fifteen minutes, repeat the procedure. It is very rough for the first few days, when people are often up five or six times a night, but eventually the body and the mind start to get the message.'

Dr Morawetz's guinea pigs were required to fill in a diary of their sleep habits for two weeks before beginning the course. Four weeks later, after it finished, they had to do the same, and again four months later to see if any gains that were made were maintained.

He divided his 150 insomniacs into various groups, the main ones being those who took sleeping pills and those who didn't. Some groups were given just the tape recording and an accompanying manual. Some had this and one-to-one sessions with Dr Morawetz. Others had the tapes supplemented by group sessions.

'For people who were not taking sleeping pills, it turned out that more than half of them had a substantial improvement in their sleep, whether they got the tape or the live therapist,' says David Morawetz, who points out that this is the first time a self-help sleep treatment has been evaluated in this way. The results were different for those insomniacs on pills. 'It turned out that there was a significant difference between those who just used the tapes and those who also had a live therapist,' he says. 'My understanding of this is that once you are taking pills there is both a physical and psychological addiction. The human contact, particularly in the groups I was running, was very helpful because people were giving each other encouragement to stay off the pills, and they had to come

back and report to each other each week how they had
done in the previous one. The people with just the tape
didn't have that. The people with the therapist or with the
groups had significantly better results, although they still
didn't do as well as those who took no pills. In retrospect,
it makes a lot of sense.'

Treating insomnia can require kid gloves. People who
reckon they are sleep deprived, for whatever reason, can
get very stroppy. Telling someone that they are expecting
too much of sleep and that they might do better with less
can bring down the furies. Psychologist Ray Meddis, who
questions the restoration theory of sleep, and who has
been searching for a happy non-somniac, got one letter in
response to his request that began: 'Sir, you are a bloody
idiot.' The writer, who said he had been going four and six
nights without sleep, went on: 'Somebody should catch
hold of you, tie you up and make you go a week without
sleep. Then see how you feel. You are supposed to be a
psychologist. In my opinion you are a bloody nut case. A
menace to society. Sleep that off.'

Perhaps the fellow felt so good after venting all this
spleen that he was able to get off to sleep. Certainly
lowering tension, anger and frustration eases the
insomniac's path, and many people have peculiar ways of
doing so. One insomniac man reported to a sleep disorder
centre in the US that the most effective step for him when
he woke in the middle of the night was to get up and take
an icy cold bath. Others have found that writing poetry,
particularly when it is soft and warm, is soporific.
Undoubtedly many of the great writers have cranked out
vast amounts on sleep, or the lack of it. William Wordsworth had terrible trouble nodding off. Several of his
miscellaneous sonnets could be called somnets, dedicated

as they are 'To Sleep'. In one published in 1807 his imagery seems very tired:

> This tiresome night, O Sleep! thou art to me
> A fly, that up and down himself doth shove
> Upon a fretful rivulet, now above,
> Now on the water vexed with mockery.

In another sonnet, written after three sleepless nights, Wordsworth said that he had tried many of the insomniac's traditional methods, including 'a flock of sheep that leisurely pass by one after one, the sound of rain and bees murmuring, the fall of rivers, winds and seas, smooth fields, white sheets of water and pure sky'. No luck:

> Could not win thee, Sleep, by any stealth
> So do not let me wear tonight away:
> Without Thee what is all the morning's wealth?
> Come, blessed barrier between day and day,
> Dear mother of fresh thoughts and joyous health!

Although, to some, the thought is not fresh or joyous, Wordsworth might have tried sex (either with his wife Mary or his girlfriend Annette) rather than scenic imagery as a road to sleep. Sex has been shown to be one of the surest cures of insomnia. Here it must be added, however, that the converse can apply, unfulfilled sexual arousal being a painfully powerful road to wakefulness.

Most sleep researchers warn against heavy physical exercise late at night, because it gets the body going rather than slowing, but sexual activity is an exception. A physically sated, loving couple on a good mattress is a perfect recipe (although it should be added that a post-coital cigarette is out; nicotine and sleep are not compatible.) Where circumstance or choice lead to people sleeping solo, many medicos are not only condoning masturbation as a sleep aid, they are actively encouraging it. One woman, for example, went to a sleep disorder clinic in Toronto saying her sleep was awful; she had violent nightmares, and she couldn't cope with her life. It emerged that she hadn't had any sexual experience with men and yet felt very guilty about masturbating. After doctors convinced her that this wasn't something to feel terrible about, her condition – and her sleep – improved dramatically.

Fear of sex, having it forced upon you, demanded of you, or enduring it when it is unrequited and based on heat rather than warmth, probably accounts for more sleepless nights than most other causes (it may also explain that fellow who took midnight icy baths!). Many insomniacs would probably benefit from marriage guidance and lessons in sexual communication rather than sheep counting or bottled sedation.

Married people who don't satisfy each other sexually and who lie awake worrying about it can take some solace from an article in the Melbourne *Sun* a few years ago. The story, datelined London, was that couples in double beds glow as they sleep, exchanging low-level radiation. A Professor John Fremlin was quoted as saying that everybody has 100 grams of radioactive potassium in their bodies, and a spokesman for the British National Nuclear Corporation said that tests showed that exposure to low but regular radiation levels leads to prolonged life, apparently through diminishing the risk of cancer. The professor added, however, that the benefits would not apply if the couple slept in a single bed, their closeness blocking the energy flow between their bodies.

If you are a member of a nuclear disarmament party and find the thought that your partner may be slowly irradiating you abhorrent, then perhaps you'd better forget all this and go back to counting – sheep through a gate, waves on the shore, bolts in an engine, all the school lunch sandwiches you've made in the past year. Everybody has something to count. In an op shop recently I found a thin volume called 'Music for Pleasure', a book made from talks the great British critic Neville Cardus had given on the ABC in 1946. (It is probably not Auntie's fault, but half the pages are printed upside down.) In one of the talks, Cardus was explaining how hard it was for a critic to keep a fresh outlook on that most popular of all symphonies, Beethoven's Fifth, given that he'd heard it so often. Cardus said: 'When I am unable to get to sleep at nights, I don't count sheep through a gate, I count the times I have heard the fifth symphony of Beethoven. And when I have reached 6,000 I usually fall into a profound slumber, and dream that I am hearing it for the 6001st time.'

DANGEROUS SLEEP: THE LAST SNORE

SNORING is almost grounds for justifiable homicide. The hilarity of snoring comes more with hindsight. Bill, the alcohol-dependent non-somniac mentioned earlier, says his family claims that he is one of the world's loudest and most consistent snorers. When he is having a pleasant afternoon doze, his family has to turn the television to full volume to compete.

He says: 'I have been banned from all shared accommodation, such as ski clubs, youth hostels, rooms on construction projects, and the like. When staying at friends' properties in the bush, I am always relegated to the barn, or a tent is pitched for me far from the homestead. On camping trips I have always been required to take my own sleeping equipment.

'Last year I tried to attend relaxation classes, but, just as the whole class was becoming wonderfully relaxed, the thunderous sounds from my corner would turn the class into bedlam, with some laughing uproariously and others, including the instructor, being quite angry and insulting. I was, of course, asked to attend no longer. One problem is the effect on audiences in theatres, lectures and church. My snoring not only drowns out the actors, lecturer or whatever sermoniser, but those who have not heard such snoring before think I am putting it on and, on awakening, the waves of hate are very intense.'

Most families have a snoring story – an uncle, an aunt, a cousin who has rattled the windows and registered on the Richter scale. But for some families snoring is deadly serious. Many heavy snorers suffer from what is called 'sleep apnea syndrome', apnea being the Greek word for breathless, and it means that they regularly stop breathing while they are asleep. The consequences can be disastrous.

Obstructive sleep apnea is not a medical curiosity. It used to be thought of as such and was until recently referred to as 'Pickwickian syndrome' because of Dickens's fat character, Joe, who was always eating, sleeping and snoring. Samuel Pickwick was also obese and a heavy drinker, and Dickens describes him under the influence of wine: 'His head was sunk upon his bosom and perpetual snoring, with a partial choke occasionally, were the only audible indications of this great man's presence.'

The picture of the fat, inebriated snorer slumped in his post-prandial chair has never inspired much sympathy. A far more offensive predecessor of Pickwick was a slob called Dionysius (not to be confused with the great tippler Dionysus) who was born about 360 BC. Dionysius was described by a writer called Aelianus as having 'through daily gluttony and intemperance increased to an extraordinary degree of corpulency and fatness, by reason whereof he had much ado to take breath. The physicians ordered for remedy of this inconvenience that needles should be made very long and small, which when he fell into a sound sleep should be thrust through his sides into his belly. Which office his attendants performed, and til the needle had passed quite through the fat, and came to the flesh itself, he lay like a stone; but when it came to the firm flesh he felt it and awakened'.

Why anyone bothered with this treatment, given that he was a tyrant as well as a pig, is not explained. The big butterball was quoted by another writer as saying: 'One thing for my own self I desire – and this seems to me the only death that is a happy dying – to lie on my back with my many rolls of fat, scarce uttering a word, gasping for breath, while I eat and say, "I'm rotting away in pleasure."'

No wonder snoring has got a bad name! But research into respiration and sleep disorders has taken many leaps since Dionysius rotted away and a few bounds since Dickens drew Pickwick. And two Australian doctors are at the forefront of tackling what modern medicine has dubbed sleep apnea syndrome.

Sleep apnea does not happen with all snoring. Steady, mild, rhythmical snoring is merely an announcement that air is travelling into and out of the sleeper's lungs, the noise being caused by air turbulence vibrating the pillars of the tonsils and the soft palate through a narrowed airway.

Snoring can be dangerous when there is a long, long pause between grunts. It is this silence, usually ended by a thunderous snort, with the sleeper sometimes thrashing about and then snuffling back to quietness, that is the problem.

Nicholas Saunders, professor of medicine at the University of Newcastle, and Colin Sullivan, professor of medicine at Sydney University, are the leading authorities on sleep and breathing in Australia. Professor Saunders explains what happens to the snorer who suffers obstructive sleep apnea syndrome: 'When we are awake the muscles of the upper airway, the pharynx and the tongue, all have tone or tension. These muscles get a burst of activity with every breath, maintaining the tone that keeps the airway open. Tone tends to decrease with sleep. In some people, the airway can close completely, so no air goes in or out. It is this intermittent closure that is called obstructive sleep apnea. It may be worse in some people simply because they have been born with a smaller upper airway to start with.

'What happens in these episodes is that the oxygen level in the body falls and the sleeper transiently arouses, not in the sense of being awake or conscious, but you can measure the increase in brain activity. The arousal leads to the return of tone to the airway muscles, the person snorts in air, and the sleep cycle resumes.'

Professor Saunders says that in bad cases sleep and breathing can become mutually exclusive. 'People can have more than 400 episodes of apnea in a night, enormous snorts and then a silence that can last from twenty to ninety seconds while the sleeper is literally asphyxiating. What triggers the recovery snort is not fully understood; it could be falling oxygen levels or climbing carbon dioxide levels in the blood. It's a bit like ascending Mount Everest 400 times a night without oxygen.'

Sleep apnea syndrome affects far more men than women (perhaps there's a connection here with the fact that more women than men suffer insomnia?) and worsens with age. No one yet knows how widespread it is, but it has been shown that about 30 per cent of men between the ages of forty and fifty snore heavily and habitually, and it is estimated that 20 per cent of them may have significant sleep apnea, although most of them won't know it. Professor Saunders says: 'The prevalence is at least 1 per cent to 4 per cent of the middle-aged male population and may be substantially higher, particularly in the elderly. This high prevalence in the elderly may explain the frequent complaints of fatigue, "lack of pep" and sleep disturbance.'

It is this fatigue and excessive daytime sleepiness that is the main consequence of sleep apnea syndrome. And because the sufferer breathes quite normally when awake and has no conscious knowledge of what he or she goes through each night, the condition is frequently not diagnosed. Professor Saunders says sufferers are often identified by talking to their bed partner. 'The major symptoms, snoring and daytime sleepiness, are rarely volunteered by the patient.' He describes the daytime sleepiness as 'severe enough to interfere with effective functioning'. Drivers may fall asleep at the wheel while waiting for traffic lights to change. Industrial accidents and absenteeism are common. Sexual failure can cause problems at home.

It is not known whether the excessive daytime sleepiness that afflicts the apnea sufferer is caused by partially waking up so many times a night, or whether it is a consequence of reduced oxygen in the blood because the sleeper isn't breathing enough. Either way, life can be hell for an apnea sufferer, and his or her family. The victims can spend their nights shaking the neighbourhood and their days in a zombie-like state. As it turns out, they don't have to be fat imbibers like Pickwick or the grotesque Dionysius. Take the case of Tom Fogarty, who lives in West Geelong, Victoria.

'You could hear Tom's snoring three blocks away,' Kath Fogarty, his wife, says. 'I remember when we had three small children and I'd have to get up when they were teething and so on, in the night. I was so tired at this time because of the babies that I was pretty cross with Tom for all the noise he made. He used to say, " I can't help it." I feel bad now that I know what Tom was going through, but I didn't know then that he was stopping breathing between his snorts. We'd had a double bed in the middle of the room but because of his snoring we switched to two single ones against the walls. Our daughter tells me that she used to lie awake waiting for her father to hit the wall as he thrashed about for breath.

'He was steadily getting worse. In 1972 we were driving back from Ballarat when Tom fell asleep at the wheel of the car. Luckily I was able to grab it before we crashed, but from then on Tom didn't do any distance driving.

'I went back to teaching, and I suppose I didn't notice that there was a gradual deterioration in Tom's health. He was going to sleep more and more. In a way, looking back, it was like a drought; the further you go the worse it gets. By about 1980 I was fearfully worried. He seemed to be dying in front of me. He was sleeping all the time. I took over all the paperwork, cheques, etcetera. Then Tom was offered a job as a reservoir keeper at Lovelybanks, which meant him living on the premises. We had six children in various stages of being educated at this stage, so he went to the job and we stayed on at our house. I really thought at the time that Tom would be dead within six months.

'There was a great strain on the marriage, of course. Communication broke down – you would go to say something to Tom and he would be asleep. The kids would race into the house from outside to say, "Hey Dad! Oh, never mind, go back to sleep." So they would come to me.

'The pressure came to a head in about June 1982. Tom was on holidays and he seemed to be sleeping nearly twenty-four hours a day. I remember asking him to get the steps and to get a big saucepan down from the cupboard so I could make jam. The phone rang just as he got it. Ten minutes later I returned from the phone, and there he was

SNORE

TANDBERG

up the steps, still holding the pan. He couldn't think what to do with it.'

Kath Fogarty knew that her husband's sleep was in a mess and that he was suffering physically and mentally from it, but she couldn't find a doctor to take it seriously. She did come across a small newspaper article quoting Professor Colin Sullivan saying that snoring could be dangerous and took it and her husband to see a GP. She says bitterly: 'The GP just said that he, too, would sleep twenty-one hours a day if he could.'

Then, by chance, Kath Fogarty saw Professor Sullivan talking about sleep apnea syndrome on television and saying that the spouse is always the one to consult because of the sleep disturbance and snoring. 'He said he was working on a device to help apnea sufferers, which he described as a cross between a gas mask and a surgical collar, but he was still in the early stages of research. I wrote to him.'

No one in Australia seems to have become very excited about it, but what Professor Sullivan had invented has become as important to apneic snorers as the bionic ear is to many deaf people. More important really, because deafness isn't life threatening. Professor Sullivan came up with a way to keep the snorer's collapsed upper airway open through the night. It's called 'continuous positive airway pressure', or 'CPAP'.

A clear plastic mask is glued over the snorer's nose, using medical latex to keep a tight seal. A hose rather like the ones used on hair dryers connects the nose mask to a small electric blower motor that sits on the bedside table. The air pressure from the blower keeps the upper airway open, forming a sort of pneumatic splint and making breathing easy.

It was in December 1982, after enduring apnea for

about fifteen years, that Tom Fogarty got to see Professor Sullivan at the Royal Prince Alfred Hospital in Sydney. 'They did sleep tests on him,' recalls Kath Fogarty. 'To them, Tom wasn't such a bad apnea sufferer. They said some of the people they'd seen were black and blue in the mornings because of lack of oxygen. Professor Sullivan noted that Tom has a narrow windpipe and a receding chin and said that this compounded his problem when he fell asleep in a chair and his head dropped to his chest.'

At Easter time in 1983 Tom Fogarty got one of Professor Sullivan's CPAP machines. 'It was marvellous, like a miracle,' says Kath. The state of his body, which has been very bad, improved dramatically. His kidneys are back to normal, so is his liver. His heart has not recovered, but that's due to the enormous amount of work it has had to do over the years; it has been under a tremendous strain. He is alive – it's incredible.'

Tom Fogarty, a tall, well-built man of sixty-two, came into the room from watching television. 'You don't realize you are going downhill so fast,' he said with a shy grin. 'I had pains in my extremities, which were put down to gout, and the ticker wasn't too good. Now I feel so good that I'm inclined to overdo things, to go at it a bit too hard.' He's trying to forget his fifteen years of permanent sleepiness. He doesn't know how he managed to hold down his job with the water board. He realizes that oxygen starvation has impaired his mind and body, but, thanks to Professor Sullivan, he and Kath can now enjoy life and each other's company. Mind you, he wasn't too happy on the night I called to interview them. As well as obstructive sleep apnea syndrome, Tom Fogarty has another cross to bear. He barracks for the ill-fated Collingwood football team. This cold evening they were playing Hawthorn and got thrashed. Not so long ago this would not have hurt Tom Fogarty so much. He would have been snoring away in his chair.

Before Professor Sullivan invented his CPAP machine, the only option for a snorer with sleep apnea syndrome, assuming he or she was lucky enough to have the condition diagnosed in the first place, was to have a tracheotomy, in which a hole is cut into the neck and a tube is poked into it, thus bypassing the problem. The hole is capped shut during the day, when the patient breathes normally, and the wound is hidden by clothing or strategically placed jewellery. At night it is unplugged and, given that the upper airway is no longer involved, there is no snoring at all. Tracheotomy, however, is major surgery, and the hole can be unsightly, causing embarrassment. As one reviewer wrote in the *British Medical Journal:* 'It would be a harsh wife and a brave surgeon who would concede tracheotomy for an otherwise asymptomatic snorer, though it would surely cure him.'

One of the loudest snorers in New South Wales resorted to having a pipe cut into his neck when he discovered he had sleep apnea syndrome. He is George Dickie, of North Richmond, a former barracks officer in the RAAF and now a property manager for a real estate agent. George, who is fifty-eight, doesn't remember snoring being a problem when he was a youngster. 'On reflection, I believe my trouble started when my nose was badly broken when I was about twenty,' he says. 'In any case, I certainly had it at the time I got married, when I was thirty-three. I take my hat off to my wife for putting up with it all our married life. When we first got married, she tried sleeping in all the different rooms in the house, but she gave up in disgust because she said the noise was so penetrating that she might as well be in her own bed. I honestly don't think she could have had a decent night's sleep for twenty years.'

George Dickie was in the RAAF for nearly thirty years and was notorious throughout the service for his snoring. 'Nobody, but nobody wanted to sleep in the rooms next to mine,' he says. 'When I went on fishing trips with my friends, the noise was so bad that they would make me sleep on my own some 200 metres from the camp. I visited various doctors, both RAAF and civilian, but always met with the same response – that nothing could be done, but that I should try not to sleep on my back. Little did they know that I snored just as badly whatever position I was in.'

Apart from being a marital and social nuisance because of the din he made while 'sleeping', George also had a constant fight to stay awake during the day. He says: 'I went to sleep while driving several times, and it is a miracle I was not killed. I found that I could not drive for more than twenty or thirty minutes at a time before I started to nod off. It was not uncommon for me to fall asleep at a red light and to be woken up and told to drive on. No doubt, my work must have suffered, but I was kept very busy as a barracks officer in the RAAF and consequently most of my sleeping was done outside working hours. It was virtually impossible for me to watch a movie on television as I would be asleep within the first few minutes, no matter how hard I tried to stay awake.'

After he had retired from the RAAF, his long-suffering wife happened to hear of Professor Sullivan's sleep research, and George Dickie arranged to have some tests done. 'He was rather surprised,' recalls George Dickie, 'because his previous patients had been overweight and, at the time, he thought this might have been a prerequisite for apnea. I was 5 ft 9 in and weighed about 11 stone 7 lb, which is more or less an average weight. In any case, the tests proved that I was holding my breath up to ninety seconds at a time and that I was in pretty poor shape. Professor Sullivan recommended a tracheotomy, which I had done in September 1980.

'The results were miraculous, and my wife and I were able to sleep peacefully for the first time in our married life. I found that where twelve hours "sleep" before the tracheotomy were nowhere near enough, seven hours sleep were now all I needed. My only problem was that the hole in my throat kept growing over and I had to keep having it rebored to enable me to insert the plastic tube, which I had to change every morning.'

In February 1982, after he'd had the trachetomy for seventeen months, Professor Sulivan suggested that George Dickie should try his CPAP machine, then in its infancy. George says of it today: 'Although it is not as convenient as the tracheotomy, I find that I get the same results from the machine and now use it nearly every night. The main problem with the CPAP device is that you have to glue the mask on. I find this a bit of a bind and am looking forward to the day when they perfect a mask that you can put on and take off at will.'

The guidelines for diagnosing sleep apnea syndrome are at least thirty episodes a night in which there is respiratory effort without airflow, each one lasting a minimum of ten seconds. But because quite a lot of Australian doctors don't seem to know much about it, and given that snoring has traditionally been a laughing matter, many sufferers may be living a nightmare, as Tom Fogarty and George Dickie were, not knowing that they can be helped. Kath Fogarty remarks: 'It's interesting that whenever I tell someone about Tom they say, "Oh, yes, my father was like that, or uncle –" '

When I first wrote about apnea in an article in the *Age* newspaper in July 1984, several people rang with variations of 'I think I've got it. Tell me more.' One American estimate puts the incidence at 3 per cent of the population, which transferred here would mean that about 465,000 Australians have some form of sleep apnea. There are three types. The main one, affecting perhaps 80 per cent of sufferers, is the one we have been talking about, 'obstructive apnea', where there is an effort to breathe but no airflow at the nose or mouth until the sufferer snorts almost awake. A second type is called 'central apnea', where there is no airflow and no effort from the respiratory system between snorts. The third type, called 'mixed apnea', is where you have a bit of both.

There are less drastic ways to treat apnea that has not reached the devastating level of Tom Fogarty's or George Dickie's. Although it used to be thought that fatness was a precondition, researchers realize that this isn't necessarily so. One US doctor claims that only 60 per cent of sufferers are overweight. For some people, dramatic relief has come with modest weight loss; in others, extreme weight loss has brought no change.

There is agreement, however, that alcohol and apnea are bedfellows. This has been shown in measurements of the amount of oxygen in apnea sufferers' blood, using a clever device called an oximeter, which is attached to the patient's ear. Professor Sullivan says: 'Normal oxygen saturation is between 90 and 95 per cent. With moderate apnea the level will drop to say 80 per cent and down to 60 per cent during dreaming (the relaxed airway being even more so in REM sleep). If a person has had a few glasses of wine or beer, the oxygen level can fall right down to 40 or 50 per cent.'

It is not clear what are the long-term effects of regularly

depressed oxygen levels at nights. Obviously there will be damage, and some doctors have raised the possibility of a nexus between apnea and senility. Professor Sullivan says: 'We don't know which is the cart and which is the horse here. It may be that as your brain deteriorates this causes more apnea, or vice versa.'

Dr Doug McEvoy, of the Royal Adelaide Hospital, raised some questions along these lines at a joint meeting of the Australian and British thoracic societies in Adelaide in 1984. Asked about a possible link between apnea and senility he said: 'My gut feeling is that many old people who snore deeply and are drowsy during the day simply don't present to us. They're sitting in nursing homes half asleep.'

Apart from alcohol, heavy snorers should also be wary of taking sedatives and hypnotics. These central nervous system depressants may be taken in the hope that they will provide the elusive 'good night's sleep', but they may have the opposite effect by increasing the number and duration of apneic episodes. Again, old people spring to mind; disturbed sleep increases with age, and so does apnea. In America, a third of all sedative or hypnotic drugs are swallowed by people over the age of sixty, yet they make up only 15 per cent of the population.

At the other end of life, there has been a lot of discussion about possible links between sleep apnea syndrome and the mysterious killer that has devastated many families called 'SIDS', or sudden infant death syndrome. The answer to SIDS is yet to be found, but one leading Australian researcher doubts that it is linked to obstructive apnea syndrome. He is Dr Neville Newman, director of neonatology at the Royal Hobart Hospital. Dr Newman says: 'It does appear that there is probably not a very strong connection in that most studies have found that infants who have had apnea do not differ from normal infants, and there is almost never a history of previous apneas in babies who subsequently become victims of SIDS. Of course, the final event is an apnea, but naturally a terminal one, and does not necessarily indicate that there have been previous episodes of apneas.' (Tasmania has a far higher percentage of SIDS deaths than other states, with an average of 4.4 deaths for every 1,000 live births between 1975 and 1981, compared to a national average of 1.6 deaths for every 1,000 live births. Apart from Tasmania's being colder than all the other states, the disparity has not been explained.)

While researchers are still looking into the long-term physical consequences of apnea, it is already known that heavy snorers are more likely than non-snorers to have heart disease and high blood pressure. A survey of 2,000 people who visited medical clinics in Ontario, Canada, found that 2.3 per cent of non-snorers had high blood pressure, while 8.8 per cent of occasional snorers had it, 12.2 per cent of those who snored nearly every night had it, and the figure climbed to 18.5 per cent for those who snored every night.

The survey, reported in the *British Medical Journal* in September 1985, found that 1.7 per cent of non-snorers had heart disease, occasional snorers had a 5.5 per cent incidence, it was 9.9 per cent for those snoring nearly every night, and 11.8 per cent for those who snored every night.

It is the right side of the apneic snorer's heart that suffers most, the side responsible for pumping the blood it receives from the main veins into the lungs, where carbon dioxide is dumped to be exhaled and a new load of oxygen is taken up. When an apneic snorer is between snorts, there is obviously no air entering the lungs. This can cause the blood vessels to tighten, which in turn makes the right side of the heart work harder to pump into these constricted areas. Eventually this can lead to an abnormally enlarged right side of the heart, what is known as 'right ventricular hypertrophy'.

No wonder an apnea sufferer feels awful each day. Apart from continuously interrupted nights, and concomitant family derision, his or her heart is working too hard, the blood carried around the body is low in oxygen, which may cause release of adrenalin and in turn high blood pressure. A survey of apnea patients at Stanford University found that 60 per cent of adults with the syndrome and 62 per cent of children had high blood pressure. (This survey also emphasized that most patients with sleep apnea syndrome are not obese and breathe normally while awake.)

Although the physical degeneration is still being measured, the social impact and the personal suffering is undisputed. When Professor Sullivan and his colleagues at the department of medicine at Sydney University first tested his anti-apnea CPAP machine, the results could be measured in very human ways.

The first trial they did (reported in the British journal *The Lancet* in April 1981) was on five patients with a long history of noisy snoring and severe obstructive sleep apnea. Each of the quintet had excessive daytime sleepiness. One of the patients had quit as a builder because he would fall asleep while working on scaffolding and while driving. Another often fell asleep during important company meetings; one lost his job as a clerk because he fell asleep at work every afternoon. Professor Sullivan reported that one of the group, a boy of thirteen, had been considered mentally retarded, but much of this retardation was secondary to his inability to stay awake at school.

Three of the five patients had already rejected the surgical solution of having a tracheotomy.

Tests on the group showed an average of sixty-two apnea episodes an hour during non-REM sleep, with the duration of each period of breathlessness averaging thirty-five seconds. (In REM sleep it averaged forty-five seconds.) The CPAP tests involved doctors making two soft plastic tubes to fit into the nostrils of each patient. These tubes were connected to a lightweight plastic pipe, and the arrangement was held on by a clear plastic mask with an elastic strap around the head. At the base of the mask, which covered only the nose, silicone rubber was used to provide a soft seal. One end of the long plastic tube was connected to a blower motor from a vacuum cleaner. This was put inside a soundproofed box to lower the noise to the level of a humming fan. The motor had a speed control, and the pressure used to push the soft palate and the tongue forward, stopping the apneic's plug effect, was measured continuously through a catheter inserted into one of the nose plugs.

Professor Sullivan reported that the continuous positive airway pressure completely prevented the upper airway blocking in each of the five patients. The blocking could be turned off and on simply by increasing or reducing the airway pressure. He said: 'The immediate response to one night of unobstructed sleep was remarkable. Each patient awoke spontaneously, was alert, and remained awake unprompted for the rest of the day. None of the patients had excessive daytime sleepiness for that day. One of the patients had been unable to stay awake for longer than a few minutes each day.' For three days before the test the patient had been asleep most of the daylight hours, with a blocked upper airway. But after the test he was able to watch television for several hours – something he had been unable to do for years.

Surprisingly, the CPAP machine was not immediately welcomed in America, where sleep study and the resources committed to it are light years ahead of those in Australia. Part of the reason for this may be that one group of American doctors tried the CPAP method and found it wanting. The three doctors, from the Cornell Medical Centre in New York, tried continuous positive airway pressure on four people with severe obstructive sleep apnea, but said that it worked for only one, a seventeen-year-old youth they described as 'mildly mentally retarded'. And even with him they reported (in the *New England Journal of Medicine* in February 1983) that he required constant nursing attention at night because he would remove the mask during sleep. The doctors said that the other three people, all adults, complained of a feeling of suffocation from the mask, with one of them, a fifty-year-old woman, feeling so bad about this that she couldn't get off to sleep on either of two nights while wearing the mask. One of the men, aged forty-seven and suffering mixed and obstructive apnea, was reported to have slept fitfully with the mask for about three hours. Then he suddenly sat up screaming and tore off the mask. Once he calmed down, he said that he had been dreaming that he was suffocating. The three doctors concluded that their, admittedly limited, experience suggested that the device 'will often fail or be impractical'.

Professor Sullivan and his colleagues answered the New York doctors a few months later, in July 1983, pointing out that they had used the mask on fifty patients, with every one of them having apnea-free nights. The blower and mask by now had a humidifier built in so that the air would not dry the patient's mouth and throat. Professor Sullivan said: 'We can only conclude that the

New York doctors were unsuccessful for technical reasons. Indeed, the fact that three of their four subjects awoke with a "choking" sensation is a sure clue to the problem – that of a circuit with a high dynamic resistance.'

It is true that going to bed with a piece of plastic glued over your nose and a hose leading to a blower motor does not sound very soothing. And some of the Australian users, such as George Dickie, do find mixing and applying the mask sealant a bore.

One Victorian apnea sufferer I interviewed, Ken Miles, a fifty-six-year-old clerk, said that he'd had a lot of trouble adjusting to the CPAP machine he had recently bought (they cost about $500, and the medical funds won't give you a rebate for them) because he felt that the air was too cold. He solved this problem cleverly by fitting a light globe inside the box that houses the blower motor by his bedside; this warms the air before it reaches his nose. Ken Miles was one of the lucky ones. His wife Beryl found out about sleep apnea syndrome through her work as a medical librarian at a big hospital.

Although sleeping with a masked man mightn't sound much fun, the wives of snorers interviewed said, without exception, that it was better than bedding down each night with someone who fluctuated from deathly silence to nasal thundering that would tumble the walls of Jericho, and who might also give you a black eye as he thrashed awake for a desperately needed breath of air. As for sex, that is performed while awake, when breathing is not a problem and the mask is not worn. For the undiagnosed and untreated apneic snorer and his bedmate, on the other hand, sex can soon become a memory – he is simply too tired all the time.

One remarkable approach to helping snorers has been taken by a woman with no medical qualifications, Judy

Challen, who lives at Echuca on the Victoria-New South Wales border. She is an artist; her husband Graeme is a dentist. Graeme is also an A grade, triple-certificated super snorer, a cordless ghetto blaster. In the sort of Jack Spratt way that happens so often in marriage, Judy Challen happens to be a naturally light sleeper. Thus she would frequently be sitting up wide awake in bed while he would trumpet like a train in a tunnel after long, silent pauses.

Judy Challen would get out her sketch book and draw her husband, noting as she did so in which positions his snoring seemed to improve or worsen. 'Over many months of sketching I worked out that when Graeme's head, neck and shoulders were in a straight alignment he snored very lightly,' she says. 'When his head was thrown back or sideways, there was a much smaller aperture.'

With her first-hand experience and sketches, and her dentist husband's advice on anatomy and respiration, Judy Challen set about designing a pillow that would keep a snorer's head in the optimum position. Her main tools were large blocks of foam, an electric carving knife and glue. Unlike most sleep researchers, she had the great advantage of living with her guinea pig.

That was in October 1982. Many visits to the drawing board later, Judy Challen came up with specifications for a pillow that supports the sleeper's head under the neck, raises the head slightly, and tapers in a wedge shape down to almost nothing some fifteen centimetres below the shoulders.

'Graeme was obviously an apnea sufferer,' she says. 'He had such heavy snoring, the long pauses in between, plus excessive daytime sleepiness. I think he diagnosed himself as having apnea. I'm not claiming that my pillow cures apnea, Graeme still does occasionally get attacks of it, but the incidence is drastically reduced.'

Certainly a lot of snorers seem to like Judy Challen's pillow. It went on the market under the brand name 'Silent Knight' in September 1984 and just over a year later more than 60,000 of them had been sold in Australia (the recommended retail price is $39.95). The pillow won the Vicorian 'Inventor of the Month' award from the Australian Association of Inventors in December 1983, and it was one of eleven Australian inventions chosen to compete against brainstorms from all over the world in Geneva. Judy Challen's pillow took the bronze medal in the section for medical inventions.

Today, she has a Telex machine in her Echuca house and exports her pillows to several countries.

'I don't make any sweeping claims, and I emphasize to people that they should always have medical reasons for snoring examined,' she explains. 'But it's nice for me to know that out of all the pillows that have been sold fewer than 100 have been returned by people who didn't like them.' She's pleased that several doctors have asked her for samples. 'I've had so many letters from people, and more than 1,500 phone calls,' she says. 'I remember one man ringing and having the distinct feeling that he was kidding me, given that people love to make jokes about snoring. He didn't sound very old, maybe in his thirties, but he'd said that his snoring had been so bad that he and his wife hadn't slept together for six years. I was sure he was a young fellow having me on, but he kept talking about what the pillow had done for him. Then I discovered that it was no joke. He burst into tears.'

Judy Challen has ploughed most of her royalties from the pillow into her export campaign (she's also had to take legal action to protect her invention), but what money she does make she plans to put into her next medical invention.

For some snorers whose problem is polyps or other physical obstruction, surgery may be the answer. In America, snorers are able to get the equivalent of a facelift inside their upper airway. Known as 'uvulo plato pharandectomy', the operation tightens everything up and prunes back fatty tissue. But Australian authorities such as Professor Sullivan and Professor Saunders have expressed reservations about this drastic step because it is hard to reverse, there may be dangers from scar tissue and there is not yet enough data to satisfy them that snorers will benefit from it.

Meanwhile, most snoring is still treated as a joke. It is denied at dinner parties and denounced over breakfast. But should Tom Fogarty have had to wait fifteen years before, by chance, his wife got a clue to his devasting sleepiness? And how many elderly people in nursing homes are labelled senile because they are 'trying to climb Mount Everest' hundreds of times each night? The thought brings to mind the old nursery rhyme:

> It's raining, it's pouring,
> the old man's snoring.
> He went to bed and bumped his head
> and couldn't get up in the morning.

We're not told how he bumped his head or why he felt so bad next morning, but he may have been struggling through the night under the weight of sleep apnea syndrome.

One Melbourne doctor who runs the respiratory unit at a big public hospital says: 'Although respiratory problems are the second most common cause of general hospital admissions (after cardio-vascular) and the most common in children's hospitals, they have not attracted the research funds that, say, cancer has. People tend to think sleeping and breathing are a bit airy-fairy; it's a very under-recognized, low-priority area. For example, I have one of Colin Sullivan's machines, but I don't have the facilities or staff to do proper clinical testing and follow-through.'

It's unlikely that people are going to start wearing 'Save the Snorers' T-shirts or putting 'Nobody Nose the Trouble I've Seen' bumper stickers on their cars, but perhaps they deserve more help than derision. Mark Twain wrote in *Tom Sawyer Abroad*, 'There ain't no way to find out why a snorer can't hear himself snore.' Although they might be oblivious to it, the price paid by many nocturnal trumpeters can be extremely high.

I MUST HAVE BEEN DREAMING
WHEN I MARRIED HIM

ANNOYING SLEEP: THE PARASOMNIAS

PARASOMNIAS have nothing to do with sleepy soldiers from the parachute regiment. They are, however, a small army of nocturnal invaders. To continue the military analogy, they are a bit like MASH: there is the hilarity of Radar O'Reilly or Klinger, but the background is the bloody reality of the Korean war.

The parasomnias include sleepwalking, talking, night terrors, bruxism (or teeth-grinding), nocturnal epilepsy, sleep-related bedwetting, and head banging.

It has been estimated that 5 per cent of the population have some form of parasomniac disorder, about 760,000 Australians. Because, in most cases, parasomnias are not life threatening, they show up less in sleep research centres than do excessive sleepiness or insomnia.

Before discussing some of the parasomnias, it may be useful to give an idea of how a sleep centre works. There are more than forty in the US, mainly attached to big hospitals, and well over a hundred doctors and other specialists have been certified by examination of the Association of Sleep Disorder Centres. There is no such supervisory body in Australia, mainly because it takes more than one to associate, and our only fully fledged hospital sleep laboratory is the one run by Professor Colin Sullivan at Sydney's Royal Prince Alfred. This is an obvious reflection of the low priority given here to sleep studies, despite the 'average' person spending twenty-two years of his or her life asleep. For many years Professor Sullivan's sleep unit was run, as one of his colleagues puts it, 'out of a cupboard', and today its funding comes not from the hospital but from the National Health and Medical Research Council, Sydney University, and whatever other bequests and grants that can be scrounged. 'We are still looking for a sugar daddy,' says one of the research staff.

Professor Sullivan started the unit in 1979, but it was only in July 1984 that it got fixed premises. His domain is now squashed into the end of a general ward on the tenth floor of the Page Chest Pavilion, an ageing wing of the Royal Prince Alfred. The sleep unit usually has a motel-like sign hanging on the door saying, 'Quiet, sleep studies in progress.' Inside, the four bedrooms lead off a small central office crammed full of recording equipment and computer terminals. In 1979-80, the makeshift set-up made eighty-four sleep studies; in 1984-85, the unit did 631. To give some scale to these figures, about four years ago, eleven US sleep disorder centres pooled their records to get a better idea of the incidence of various problems. That aggregate came to 39,000 patients. (About half the total were seen because of disorders of excessive sleep; about one-third had some sort of insomnia.)

A sleep study is expensive. Apart from the possible involvement of consultants in respiratory medicine, cardiologists, neurologists, urologists, psychologists and psychiatrists, there must be nursing staff, lots of monitoring equipment, and polysomnographics technicians to run it. One patient's continuous electroencephalogram, or recording of brain activity, can produce as much as 450

metres of paper printout in a single night. At least eight
electrodes are attached to the patient in a routine sleep
study. Two are placed on the central scalp. Two are put
just either side of the sleeper's eyes for an electrooculo-
gram, or recording of eye movement. Another pair is
placed below the chin to give an electromyogram, or
muscle readings. A further two reference electrodes go on
the ear lobes. A device called an oximeter can also be
attached to the ear to show blood oxygen levels. Other
sensors and measurers can be placed on just about any
part of the body, and closed-circuit television cameras and
sound recorders monitor movement and snoring.

The equipment used depends on what the researchers
are looking for, given that people referred have already
had various form of assessment, including interviews and
have usually kept a sleep diary for some time before they
reach the laboratory. One useful device is a strain gauge,
which can record, for example, respiratory effort by
following the movements of muscles involved in breathing. A strain gauge can even be used to record erections
during sleep, or 'nocturnal penile tumescence', as
researchers coyly call them. This is done not out of
voyeurism but to help to determine possible causes of
impotence. All normal men have erections during REM
sleep. This happens quite irrespective of dream content. A
man will have erections in REM sleep even if he is
dreaming of sitting naked on a polar ice floe. So if an
impotent patient in a sleep laboratory has no erections
during a night's recording, the cause of his problem is
likely to be physiological; if he does have erections in his
REM sleep but is impotent when awake, his problem is
likely to be psychological. Thus a simple, painless sleep
study can save enormous amounts of diagnostic time and

the patient shuffling between urologist and psychiatrist (even if going to a shrink for impotence sounds like a contradiction!).

Fortunately, penile problems are one of the rarer parasomnias that sleep laboratories have to deal with. But there are plenty of others. When, in 1985, I wrote an article in the *Age* about dream interpretation, I asked readers to tell me about their dreams and sleep habits. Many of the dozens of letters I got concerned parasomnias. My favourite came from 'Heather H', who lives at Lakes Entrance, in eastern Victoria. She had no trouble sleeping, apart from a certain nervousness about what her husband might get up to next. His problem was that his dreams were so vivid that he acted upon them. She explains:

'Once he physically moved the furniture around in the bedroom, making it impossible to walk out the door. He was totally asleep. I woke up and asked him what he was doing, told him to get back into bed and go to sleep. In the morning, he was totally unaware of his actions, despite the fact that the furniture is rather heavy. Another time I woke up in a headlock. He was dragging me out of the bed and on to the floor. His grip was hard to release. In the morning, he said he had dreamt we were in a car accident and he was trying to get me out of the car.

'Another time I woke up and all the covers were off. My husband was brushing me off and talking about ants covering me. He had no recollection of this in the morning.

'Recently he got out of bed in his sleep and went out on to the front lawn going through the motions of mooring our yacht, including yelling instructions. In the morning, half asleep, he got up to check that the yacht was still moored. He could recall the dream but not getting out of bed.'

Apart from moving furniture, clamping his wife in headlocks and brushing imaginary ants from her sleeping body, 'Heather H's' husband also likes to chat in his sleep. She says: 'He talks a lot, sitting upright and starting the conversation. I can talk to him and discuss things. Sometimes I don't realize that he is asleep because he seems so awake. At other times I just tell him to stop and to go back to sleep. Usually he does.

'I have tried to link his sleeping habits with social factors. I used to think they occurred when he'd had long work hours and was tired, but that doesn't seem to fit. When he has been relaxed and not under a lot of stress he still behaves this way. I find it humorous now, except that sometimes it is hard to get back to sleep after he wakes me up, as I am left wondering.'

Bizarre though 'Heather H's' nights may be, she is not alone. Another woman rang me to talk of her father's lifelong sleepwalking. 'Mum would wake up in the middle of the night and Dad would be pushing the bed, with her in it, across the room. He'd say that he was getting her away from the fire that, in his dream, was burning down the house. Mum had to put a padlock and chain on the front door at nights to stop him walking off down the street in his pyjamas. Once an enormous crash came from their bedroom in the night. Dad had pulled a big wardrobe down on himself. He had to have six stitches in his head. He'd been trying to climb up the wardrobe, a big old one on legs. Later he told us that he'd been dreaming that he was climbing a spiral staircase.'

Another correspondent, a twenty-five-year-old woman, wrote about her own sleepwalking, which she described as frightening: 'I have only woken once during a walk, but there is plenty of evidence of me walking at other times. Once I woke up to find myself wearing gumboots and trying to put on overalls over my nightie. I fell over in the process, waking myself up. I was wearing my glasses and a beanie and was getting ready to milk the cows. As we have always lived in towns and never on a farm, this was quite disconcerting.

'Many mornings I have woken up and not been aware that I have walked during the night until I find such things as grass between my toes, doors open and my glasses and dressing gown in rooms other than my bedroom, where I leave them each night. My mother has told me that I walked frequently when I lived at home. One night my parents stopped me and asked me where I was going, and I replied clearly that I was going to Grandma's – a distance of 37 kilometres. Mum has said that I was always coherent when sleepwalking and easily steered back to bed if I was told quietly that I could go where I was going later.' She could not recall her walks and was highly sceptical about them until the time she fell over and woke as she was about to go and milk the imaginary cows.

What seems most surprising is that we don't hear of more sleepwalkers hurting themselves. Presumably this is because a lot of them are steered back to bed by parents or partners. Obviously single sleepwalkers need to avoid tall buildings, and should lock doors and windows and put away potentially dangerous objects before going to bed. Some sleepwalkers tie a rope loosely around their waist, the end attached to a bedpost. The theory is that as the rope tightens the walker is aroused, but some sleepwalkers learn to untie the rope before strolling.

Here lies one of the clues to somnambulism, although there is no clear answer, or cure. Sleepwalking seems to rise from a confused mixture of sleep and wakefulness. When we are awake, our brain emits alpha waves; when in deep sleep it gives out delta waves. The sleepwalker has a bit of both wave patterns, so he or she can almost be said to be awake and asleep at the same time. Because they are 'awake', the walkers can perform various uncomplicated tasks (like untying the restraining rope), but because they are 'asleep', they usually do not remember having walked.

The traps into which these unclear brainwaves can lead the sleepwalker were demonstrated by two Swiss brothers who were staying in a boarding house while their parents went away on holiday. During the night the younger of the boys started sleepwalking. The older brother woke and followed to see that he came to no harm. The young boy walked to the door of the bedroom of the couple who owned the boarding house, opened it, went in and climbed across the recumbent and very large figure of the wife, settling back to deep delta sleep in between her and her husband. Neither of the owners woke up. The poor older brother stared in horror. What was he to do? If he woke them, how would he explain his brother's presence, or for that matter his own, in the bedroom? On the other hand, what would become of little brother if he did nothing and the man happened to wake to find another person snuggled between himself and his wife? It was like a real-life Swiss version of that old Speedy Gonzales joke, in which the husband, having heard that the randy little Mexican was in town, reached over in the night to put a reassuring hand on his wife, only to hear: 'Who has hees hand on ze bum of Speedy Gonzales?' In the end, the poor older brother decided that discretion was the better part of squalor and slunk back to his own bedroom. No doubt he couldn't go back to sleep, but his decision was the right one. About half an hour later the younger brother walked back to their room, again in his sleep, and got back into his own bed. No one was the wiser.

Although sleepwalking tends to come and go with children (and it has been shown in laboratories that many will walk if lifted up and put on their feet during delta sleep), it is regarded as more significant in adults, perhaps related to stress. Behaviour therapy, hypnosis and various drugs have been used on adult walkers, but with mixed results. Where nothing seems to work, the only 'treatment' is to ensure that the sufferer comes to no harm by locking doors and windows and making sure that keys are at hand for the bed partner in case of fire.

There does appear to be a family history with many walkers. Another woman who wrote about her habits is a twenty-seven-year-old mother of two who lives at Ferny Creek, in Victoria. 'Sue W' says: 'All my life I have been a walker, talker, doer or active dream sleeper, and my husband claims to be able to carry on conversations with me, although only on the subject I was dreaming of at the time. Any intervention by him usually results in me stating emphatically my point on the subject.'

Knowing his wife's habits, 'Sue W's' husband once rigged up an alarm system on the front door of their flat because he was going overseas and he feared that she might come to harm. 'The battery-operated alarm was meant to sound if the door was opened,' 'Sue W' recalls. 'Unfortunately one night I found myself freezing cold sitting on the concrete stairs outside the flat with the buzzer still going. If the door had slammed, I would have been marooned in my nightie. I'm not sure how long I was there.'

Today, with two young children, she finds that her

dreams are based on the day's events with her family, and this in turn weaves into her walking. 'One very cold night we went to bed early,' she writes. 'About 1 am I dreamt that my fourteen-month-old daughter Erica had been violently sick all over me, my husband and the bed. I "woke" wringing wet and smelling awful. I grabbed a clean nightie and leapt under the shower. Then I *really* woke up. By the time I got back into bed I was frozen, and the consequence of this night jaunt was a very bad cold.' It is interesting that 'Sue W' didn't have a cold shower; she managed to adjust the taps in her sleep, waking only when the water hit her skin. She adds: 'My son Robert, who is three, is a very "disturbed" sleeper and walks about, not knowing where he is when he wakes. Erica, too, is showing restless tendencies. Can my huband survive with three of us in the family?'

'Living out' dreams can be more worrying than imagining that you've been puked upon. 'Carolyn B', an articulate young woman who lives on the Mornington Peninsula, in Victoria, wrote about her dream-related experiences, as she called them.

'Although I have not had any violent dreams lately, I have in the past woken in the night to find myself bashing into my bedroom wall as if possessed. On one occasion, while travelling overnight on a bus, I was told that I tried to strangle my companion while sleeping. These types of occurrences, sleep walking, and so on, go back over many years. I have often thought they resulted form a mental disturbance, which in turn was due to experiences in my youth with the loss of my right eye in an accident when I was six, and the death of my mother a year later. I feel that I have overcome the pain of these events, but my dreams seem to suggest that this is not so. When I have woken screaming and shivering with fear in the middle of the night, I cannot always remember the dream, but I have this feeling of helplessness and terror. These "nightmares" began when I was in hospital when I lost my eye, with my belief in the existence of a mechanical monster outside my ward. I believed that this monster existed in reality (the monster within?), and I still remember how it looked and moved. The vividness of these dreams startles me on reflection as I can recall actually writhing at the pain of being stabbed in the back in one of my dreams. The morning after an active night's dreaming I feel worn out and irritable, as if I'd hardly slept at all. I still feel that I have no control over these dreams, and I have tentatively accepted them as an over-active subconscious in which my thoughts are manifested in my dreams.'

It should be said that, despite the gripping fear and violence of her nights, 'Carolyn B', does not appear to be an acutely depressed woman. She asks: 'How can we ever define the barrier between conscious and unconscious when the capabilities of the mind are not known? As we enter the grey area between the real and unreal it seems like the last great frontier.' She signs off, 'Regards and sunshine.'

The violence and headbanging she inflicts or suffers are likely signs of suppressed emotional stress. Sleep-related headbanging is labelled 'jactatio capitis nocturna' and is more common in children than adults. Some children and adults also rock their head or body just before or during sleep, again thought to be a reaction to emotional stress.

Another parasomnia is the night terror. It can be distinguished from an ordinary nightmare in several ways. Nightmares happen in REM sleep, usually towards the end of the night when we are having the longest of the dreaming spells that together occupy about ninety minutes

of the 'normal' night. Night terrors, however, usually spring from non-REM stages, and are common in the early part of sleep, especially the first hour or two. They differ also in that they contain a shorter, simpler scene than a nightmare, which, as we all know, can be frighteningly detailed.

This isn't to say night terrors are not vivid; quite the contrary. The sufferer will often sit up in bed screaming his or her lungs out, sweating profusely, heart pounding, gasping for breath. An example is Robyn Rodick, a twenty-five-year-old telephonist from the Sydney suburb of Hornsby. Most sufferers of night terrors, like sleep walkers, usually know little about what they have been through by the time morning has come around. Robyn's mother, Pat Rodick, explains: 'Robyn works on the international switchboard on permanent night shifts. She is okay when she sleeps during the day. It is when she has a day off and sleeps at night that she has the attacks.'

Pat Rodick, who is a medical secretary, says the terror attacks begin with Robyn breathing quickly, then really catching her breath, gasping with fright – then the screaming starts. Fortunately the Rodicks have a vacant block on one side of their house, and the neighbour's house on the other side is built in such a way that it doesn't get the full blast of Robyn's screams.

'We have told the neighbours around us so that they don't imagine rape or murder being committed,' Pat Rodick says. 'They say it's not a problem, but I think they are being kind. Certainly all the neighbourhood dogs take on and all start barking when they hear the noise. Once we stayed in a caravan park, where Robyn and her brother Mark shared one tent and my husband and I were in another. In the middle of the night, Robyn began to scream blue murder. The owner of the caravan park came running with his Alsatian, and people were coming from everywhere armed with sticks and other weapons. It's funny to look back on, but it was pretty embarrassing at the time.'

Sometimes Robyn Rodick screams so hard that blood vessels in her throat burst and she has to go to the bathroom to spit out blood.

'The attacks are mainly in the first hour after she has gone to sleep,' Pat Rodick says. 'She's had up to three episodes a night. Sometimes I feel that I can predict an attack, usually when Robbie has nights off work and has gotten tired, or when she is under emotional stress. There is a strain on the whole family because you are waiting for it to happen. One of us has to rush to her room when it does. The first thing you do is put the light on. Robbie's eyes will be open, but you have to bring her back to reality. Often I've sat with her on the end of the bed for ten or fifteen minutes. It is so sad to see; she is in such a state of terror.'

The image at the heart of Robyn Rodick's terror is always the same, and is simple: hands are reaching out to get her. It is some unknown, terrifying intent behind these grasping hands that electrifies her mind and body with fear and provokes the bloodcurdling screams.

Sleep terror attacks are much more common in children than adults. No one really knows what is behind them, although some researchers regard childhood night terrors as a relatively insignificant stage of the developing sleep pattern, with adult ones being more serious, perhaps outgrowths of a problem such as anxiety, extreme agitation, or inhibition of aggression. Whether or not night terrors can be associated with a singular terrifying event is not clear, although the Rodicks think this may be the case with Robyn. About 6.30 one November morning in 1980,

Robyn was driving home along the Warringah freeway after a night's work at the international telephone exchange. The streets were not crowded and Robyn was not particularly sleepy, but suddenly a moth flew in the window and into her face. Robyn reefed the steering wheel, lost control, and the car smashed into a huge stanchion. She was badly hurt: fractured sternum, broken arms, legs, kneecaps, and gashes that eventually needed plastic surgery. The police had to cut her out of the bent car, during which time Robyn drifted into and out of consciousness.

'It wasn't until a couple of years later that we twigged to a possible connection between the crash and the night terrors,' says Pat Rodick. 'Mark asked Robbie if she remembered the hands reaching out for her inside the wrecked car. She said she did. I think Mark was trying to be autosuggestive, pointing out that these hands could be seen as reaching out to help, not to harm her.'

Robyn was referred to the sleep unit run by Professor Sullivan at the Royal Prince Alfred. 'He was terrific,' says Pat Rodick. 'He helped enormously just by talking to Robyn and explaining to her that she wasn't a freak, that other people suffered night terrors.'

By mid 1985 Robyn Rodick appeared to be gradually shrugging off the attacks, which were steadily growing further apart.

A more typical case than hers is that of Denise Beale, of the Melbourne suburb of Wantirna, whose story shows the familial nature of night terrors, and their frequent association with other parasomnias, such as walking. She writes mainly of her son:

'All his life he has suffered badly from night terrors, almost from birth. As he got older he had them whenever he was upset, over-tired, over-excited, or getting sick. He also had them particularly badly when he was teething, at one stage every night for eight weeks. When he started kindergarten he had them every night for a month. They lasted between five and twenty minutes and were always eerie and distressing, though he seemed to have no consciousness of them (however, I always felt they cast a shadow over him the next day). His sleeping generally was very poor. At five he is beginning to sleep through the night (as a young child he averaged about eight wake-ups a night), but still not regularly. He often has vivid nightmares, although his night terrors are less frequent. He talks in his sleep a lot and is generally very easily disturbed. He is quite highly strung, very active, with a vivid imagination, and doesn't need a lot of sleep.'

You can see from this why sleep researchers, particularly when looking at children, place so much emphasis on spouse and family observation; a summary such as Denise Beale's, based on the closeness only a mother can know, provides the empirical evidence without which laboratory testing is of little use. The information she offers about herself is also revealing: 'I, too, have suffered all my life from night terrors. Particularly in my teens and early twenties, I would scream in my sleep every two or three months, but would wake with no memory of it. Now, I find that these night terrors are brought on only in one set of circumstances; that is, if I sleep in an entirely dark room, blinds and doors shut. Then I apparently scream in my sleep because I wake up with my throat still vibrating, shaking violently, terrified without knowing why, and not knowing who I am or where I am. Of course, I'm careful to avoid these circumstances; it just occasionally happens by accident.

'As well as that, I've been an insomniac for years (something I don't even worry about any more), grind my teeth in my sleep when I'm tense, talk in my sleep, sit upright, and very occasionally walk in my sleep. I have a lot of nightmares and many vivid dreams.'

Sometimes it isn't easy to distinguish between night-mare and night terror without the benefit of sleep laboratory observation. Val Williams of Para Hills West, in South Australia, remains puzzled to this day about a recurring dream-terror that plagued her childhood for about eighteen months. 'My conviction about nightmares is that they are outlets for fear,' she says. 'What I don't understand is *why*. I suffered the same nightmare count-less times. It was a vision of me in a room with high walls and not even a window. Apart from my own bed and wardrobe, it was otherwise bare. In the nightmares, I was in bed, next to my wardrobe, feeling extremely lonely. Suddenly, appearing above me, was a heavy blackness. As this mass slowly descended, there was a giant double scoop leading the way (towards my head). Always at that point I woke, screaming and shaking with fear. I was unable to describe in my limited English a convincing picture or at least a descriptive picture of what I had just experienced. So, after each of these frightening experi-ences, I spent the remainder of the night trying to finish my sleep in bed with Mum and Dad.'

Children like the young Val Williams are more frequent sufferers from nightmares than are adults because they spend more time in REM sleep. (It could be argued logically that they should therefore be less susceptible to night terrors, which arise from non-REM sleep, but this isn't so). The child's limited life experience also leaves him or her wider open to irrational fears of boogeymen and shadows and, say, the thump on a tin roof that a parent can put down to a possum. There is also the fear stimulus of separation from parental love and protection that bedtime involves. Bedtime rituals to reinforce in the child's mind that the separation is temporary, that parents don't disappear with darkness, can include stories, songs and tight tucking-in. My own kids grew up on extremely badly sung versions of Michael Finnegan (there being more than one because I could never remember the right words or the correct verse sequence). I always got the first one:

> There was an old man called Michael Finnegan
> He grew whiskers on his chinnegan,
> The wind came out and blew them innegan,
> Poor old Michael Finnegan.

but thereafter there was a fair bit of adlibbegan, especially if the summons to perform the bedtime ritual interrupted the proceedings of an alcoholic dinner table.

Another top of the bedtime pops was Granddad's version of the bullfrog who lived in a well and had such a cold that he couldn't sing. Whether these watery tunes (Michael Finnegan has some trouble fishing) prompted adverse autosuggestion I don't know, but one of my three children regularly had nightmares about crocodiles and regularly wet his bed.

Parents wrenched from their sleep by offspring wailing about crocodiles or monsters face the difficult choice of welcoming the child into their own warm nest or getting up, comforting and reassuring, and carrying it back to the scene of the 'crime', its own bed. The former is the soft option, but failure to establish that your bed is yours, and theirs is theirs, can have long-term side-effects.

Like night terrors, another non-REM parasomnia is nocturnal enuresis, or bedwetting. Despite the often-held view that it is a last-minute failure to arise in time to empty the night's full bladder, it usually happens during the first third of the night in stages of delta sleep. There is a theory that it is a problem of partial arousal, that although the child is unaware that he or she is wetting the bed, at the time the youngster is close to the surface of wakefulness. After wetting he (it *is* more common in males) will slide back into deep sleep and be hard to rouse. At the age of five about 10 per cent of girls and 15 per cent of boys are likely to be bedwetters. The problem rarely lasts with females, but the incidence among US navy recruits for World War II has been estimated at between 1 and 3 per cent. Whether having to fight a war is a causal factor is not mentioned, although the prospect of getting my own head blown off inspires fears not just of enuresis but also encopresis, a more solid problem.

Little is understood about this embarrassing parasomnia, and it's not hard to find contradictory 'experts'. The deep-sleep, early-night hypothesis is discarded by some researchers, who produce studies to show that bedwetting happens randomly throughout the night.

The diagnostic distinction is made between 'primary' enuresis, where there have never been dry nights, and 'secondary' enuresis, where the child has managed night-time toilet training but has returned to wetting the bed again. Before labelling it either of these, doctors rule out any physical problem such as urogenital or kidney disorders, congenitally deformed bladders, or disease.

Where bedwetting does not disappear naturally with time (which it does for most children), there are three ways to tackle it, none of them certainties.

One of the most popular, because it does not involve the use of drugs and has a high success rate (75 per cent in one study), is the bell and pad method. In this, a sensitized rubber pad is put under the bottom bedsheet, a cord connecting the pad to a box that contains a bell or buzzer and a light. As soon as the urine passes through the sheet to the pad the bell or buzzer sounds and the light goes on. The child wakes, stops peeing and heads for the bathroom. Parents must also respond to the buzzer, getting up to reassure the child, help him or her to the bathroom, offer encouragement, and change the sheet for a dry one so that the system can be switched on again. In quite a short time the wet mark gets smaller and smaller as the conditioned response is reinforced, and the magic and much-wanted dry nights start happening. The system doesn't work for all bedwetters, partly because some parents can't manage or be bothered to involve themselves enough in the process, and partly because some sufferers will regress once the pad and bell are withdrawn.

Tricyclic anti-depressants are another approach, not because there is essentially a connection to depression but rather that effectiveness in controlling enuresis is a quirky side-effect of the drug. From my own family's experience, the disadvantage here, apart from a parent's natural reluctance to regularly feed a drug to a child, is that getting the dose right is difficult. Too little won't work, too much and you start getting some of the less useful side-effects of tricyclics, such as blurred vision. There is also the risk of regression after cessation, although an option here is to continue with placebo pills.

Where the damage is thought to be psychological, through inappropriate handling of toilet training in the first place or a particular trauma, such as a parent's death or divorce, some form of psychotherapy may be worth considering, although it's necessary to distinguish between a deep-seated trauma and wetting caused by transient stress, such as moving school or an isolated conflict like a row with a best friend.

Yet another approach is to look for an allergy, such as

foods high in acids or caffeine-containing drinks. As with any allergy, finding the problem-causing substance is an exhaustive process, but at least there are no side-effects, and the child has the reassuring feeling that what is being sought is something 'wrong' in a particular food or drink, rather than in him or her.

Paediatricians often proffer the reward system of gold stars for dry nights and maybe a monthly cash sum based on how many there have been. Others will suggest that the best approach is no approach, that you should keep the lowest possible profile and make no fuss whether the child is wet or dry. Some will recommend that the child has no fluid, especially drinks containing citric acid, after a certain hour; others say let them drink what they like.

A less worrying or widespread parasomnia is bruxism, or grinding the teeth. The only problem here, apart from driving a bed partner to distraction, is worn out teeth. 'Vivienne L', a twenty-five-year-old single woman who lives in Melbourne, has a qualification in organizational psychology, and works for a big company, says: 'I am not aware of grinding my teeth while I am asleep, but once awake I realize that I must have been because my teeth and gums ache. Also my teeth have been worn down. Sleeping partners over several years have commented on the forcefulness of the grinding and that in a conscious state I would be unable to grind my teeth with such vigour. I have been woken up by friends who feel I must be causing some harm to myself. Apparently I sound like a bulldozer!

'Unfortunately, I seldom remember my dreams, so I am unable to use them to shed some light on my agitation. Also, I am unable to link any event through the day to my tooth grinding; that is, I appear to be no worse at the end of a stressful day. I have noticed, however, that I am worse when I am away from home, in a different bed, while travelling, and so on. This would make sense because I'm probably more agitated in unfamiliar surroundings.'

Teeth grinding usually happens in the second stage of non-REM sleep, which disconnects it from dreaming. People who grind their teeth during the day are often reflecting stress; at night-time there is no established link to hangover stress or emotional upset, which fits with 'Vivienne L's' inability to trace a cause. All that can be said for sure about bruxism is that both males and females suffer, children more so – and it won't make you go blind. The grinding itself is a consequence of clenching and unclenching the muscles you normally use for chewing (although there's no connection with hunger, either).

Like many other parasomnias, teeth grinding is thought to be a disorder of partial awakening, which, in turn, although the sleeper may not perceive any true awakening, can perhaps be related to daytime sleepiness. If the noise created is gradually threatening a visit to the Family Court, or if the cud-like grinding is leaving sore gums or stubby teeth, a dentist can supply a plastic or rubber teeth guard, which should stop both.

A far more serious parasomnia is seizure during sleep. Some sufferers of epilepsy have attacks only while they are asleep; a survey of 645 epileptic patients in 1974 revealed that thirty-eight of them had exclusively sleeping seizures. All jerky movements during sleep, however, should not panic seizure-seeking spouses. The nocturnal myoclonus or leg jerking discussed earlier has nothing to do with epilepsy; neither does the sudden single movement of an arm or leg that some people get just before falling to sleep. These inconsequential movements are called 'hypnic jerks', and have nothing to do with flower power or Haight-Ashbury.

Really the only way to pin down sleep-related epilepsy is through watching the electrical activity on an electroencephalogram. Treatment by a neurologist may involve anti-convulsive medicine.

With the plethora of parasomnias available to wreck our nights, and the heavy brigades of insomnia or excessive somnolence, not to mention circadian chaos or the dangerous honking of the sleep apnea sufferer, is it really worth it? Is losing sleep worth losing sleep over, or would be better off in a world of perpetual wakefulness? Maybe Coleridge was right to brand sleep 'distemper's worst calamity'?

No, no, a thousand times no. Because above all these invaders, fierce though they may be, soars one of life's great pieces of magic, something that transcends, poverty, wealth, the EEC, nuclear war and parking meters: The Dream.

TANDBERG

DREAM SLEEP

ALTHOUGH MAN first slept in the Garden of Eden so long ago, it was only in 1952 that it was proved that sleep can be divided into two markedly different types. Three Americans at the University of Chicago made the breakthrough. In the best traditions of science, the discovery was almost accidental.

Dr Nathaniel Kleitman was interested to see if the slow, rolling eye movements that come just before sleep also occurred throughout the night, and, if so, whether or not there was a connection to depth of sleep. Kleitman assigned post-graduate student Eugene Aserinsky to do the watching. Aserinsky found that as well as the slow rolling movements that accompany sleep onset, the patients' eyeballs began to dart around rapidly beneath the closed lids at certain times during the night. The head of the Stanford University sleep research centre, Dr William Dement, was a second-year medical student at the time, and was asked to join the observation team. They were puzzled. Why, when a person should be out to it, would their eyeballs behave as though they were awake and at the movies?

It was from this beginning that confirmation came that sleep is not a quiescent state, a stretch of pacific water after the turbulence of waking, a time when the brain and body are just ticking over while they recuperate.

William Dement gave this strange sleep stage the prosaic name REM, for rapid eye movement, its opposite non-REM. But what did it mean, they wondered? The obvious experiment was to wake people in both REM and non-REM stages to see if there was a difference. In 1957 Nathaniel Kleitman published the first exciting results of a study in which 191 awakenings were made from REM sleep. In 80 per cent of these awakenings the subject could vividly recall dreaming at the time of arousal.

Conversely, in 160 awakenings of subjects whose recorded brain waves and still eyeballs showed that they were in non-REM sleep, there were only eleven instances (6.9 per cent) where the subject could recall dreaming. The researchers were euphoric and the young William Dement couldn't wait to demonstrate the REM-dreaming link. So he learnt how to attach electrodes to his own scalp and got another medical student to monitor the read-outs, with instructions to wake him each time he was in REM sleep.

The time came, the student aroused Dement, and he recalled no trace of a dream, only a vague curiosity about what time it was. Dement was not particularly worried, the tests they had done showed that in about a fifth of REM awakenings there isn't recall. Back he went to sleep. Again the student jolted him awake. Again nothing. After this procedure had been repeated above five times Dement was so distressed by his total lack of dream recall that he admits he actually faked a bit, pretended to the student that, yes, he had been dreaming. Tired and disappointed, Dement went to examine the polygraphic record of his sleep. To his great relief, he discovered that the monitoring student had misread the recordings and had woken him, every time, while he had been in non-

REM sleep. Suitably chastized, the student repeated the experiment the next night, waking Dement in REM stages, to be regaled with a flood of vividly recalled dreams.

Since those early days a lot has been learned about the two types of sleep. Researchers have agreed that there are stages to sleep, that we go into and out of these stages cyclically (the average cycle lasting ninety minutes), that we all dream, even if, because we chance to wake up during a non-REM period, we can't always remember having done so. But what is not known, what is as much a mystery today as it was for Adam and Eve, is *why* we dream. Are these fantasies just the detritus of the day, a mere safety valve on the pressure cooker of waking thought processes? Or are they a magical mystery tour with, at the end, the holy grail of understanding, a trip down what Sigmund Freud dubbed 'the royal road to the unconscious'? That no one knows the answer is rather a pleasant thought; a sense of wonder goes a long way.

Many before him toyed with dreams, but it was Freud who first really tried to explain formally their significance. He always said that his opus, *The Interpretation of Dreams*, was his best book, even though only 351 copies were sold in the first six years after publication, despite Freud's statement: 'Insight such as this falls to one's lot but once in a lifetime.'

His interest in dreams was stimulated in 1895 by a change of bed. In a footnote to one of his papers on neuroses, Freud wrote: 'For several weeks I found myself obliged to exchange my usual bed for a harder one, in which I had more numerous or more vivid dreams, or in which, it may be, I was unable to reach the normal depth of sleep. In the first quarter of an hour after waking I remembered all the dreams I had had during the night, and I took the trouble to write them down and try to solve them. I succeeded in tracing all these dreams back to two factors: (1) to the necessity for working out any ideas which I had only dwelt upon cursorily during the day – which had only been touched upon and not finally dealt with; and (2) to the compulsion to link together any ideas that might be present in the same state of consciousness. The senseless and contradictory character of the dreams could be tracked back to the uncontrolled ascendancy of this latter factor.'

The Interpretation of Dreams is essential for anyone interested in the subject. Some of Freud's sentences are unwieldly to the point of being soporific, but, for all that, it is a remarkable book, all 871 pages of it. Apart from his own, monumental views, Freud also reviews thinking on the subject in the second half of the nineteenth century. The Frenchman Dugas said of dreams in 1897: 'A dream is a psychical, emotional and mental anarchy; it is the play of functions left to their own devices and acting without control or purpose; in dreams the spirit becomes a spiritual automaton.'

Freud quotes his contemporary F. W. Hildebrandt: 'What astonishing leaps a dreamer may make, for instance, in drawing inferences! How calmly he is prepared to see the most familiar lessons of experience turned upside down. What laughable contradictions he is ready to accept in the laws of nature and society before, as we say, things get beyond a joke and the excessive strain of nonsense wakes him up. We calculate without a qualm that three times three makes twenty; we are not in the least surprised when a dog quotes a line of poetry, or when a dead man walks to his grave on his own legs, or when we see a rock floating on the water. . .'

Freud wrote: 'Dreams are disconnected, they accept the most violent contradictions without the least objection, they admit impossibilities, they disregard knowledge which carries great weight with us in the daytime, they reveal us as ethical and moral imbeciles. Anyone who when he was awake behaved in the sort of way that is shown in situations in dreams would be considered insane.'

But while these thinkers, and many before them, spoke disparagingly of the nonsense we're happy to accept in dreams, they were not so dismissive as to overlook the beauty and mystery of them. Hildebrandt wrote: '. . . there are few of us who could not affirm, from our own experience, that there emerges from time to time in the creations and fabrics of the genius of dreams a depth and intimacy of emotion, a tenderness of feeling, a clarity of vision, a subtlety of observation, and a brilliance of wit such as we should never claim to have at our permanent command in our waking lives. There lies in dreams a marvellous poetry, an apt allegory, an incomparable humour, a rare irony. A dream looks upon the world in a light of strange idealism and often enhances the effects of what it sees by its deep understanding of their essential nature. It pictures earthly beauty to our eyes in a truly heavenly splendour and clothes dignity with the highest majesty, it shows us our everyday fears in the ghastliest shape and turns our amusement into jokes of indescribable pungency. And sometimes, when we are awake and still under the full impact of an experience like one of these, we cannot but feel that never in our life has the real world offered us its equal.' It is this passage from Hildebrandt that should be quoted to those more modern scientists who believe that dreams are simply the waking mind's rubbish bin.

We do not fall asleep literally. It is a gentler process that rises and subsides like the sea against a wall. This exquisite period of steadily overwhelming drowsiness often includes mini-dreams, what are known as hypnagogic experiences. In these the descending sleeper may have brief flashes of nonsense as the conscious is passing the baton to the unconscious, gibberish phrases that can be recalled if noted down at the time but which otherwise spin off into the ether. Frequently hypnagogic experiences produce weird phrases that include invented words, or neologisms.

Visual images may accompany these experiences, most of which are comical. More than twenty years ago the *New Statesman* magazine in England published a collection of hypnagogic flashes, the winning one being from a London man whose drowsy head threw up:

> Only God and Henry Ford
> Have no umbilical cord.

Some other examples come from Melbourne poet and academic Chris Wallace-Crabbe, who sent me a report on an overseas trip he made, in which his dreaming and waking reactions to what he was seeing are merged beautifully. In many cases, events or mere geography stimulated strange visions. He talks about one that sprang from Switzerland: 'G arrives and the three of us head off by train to the sweet green neutrality of Switzerland, its peaks and parks and pines. One result is that politics vanish entirely from the dreamworld, though language is still hyperactive; Zurich provides me with something that might well have come from *Finnegan's Wake*:

> Le black means water, especially on teeth,
> and Herr Fils means desert boots rolled up.'

A more intelligible 'flash' that crept into Chris Wallace-Crabbe's head came after he had just arrived in Jerusalem after ten days of driving around Uttar-Pradesh in India.

> I would have thought anyone would be glad to
> give a man shekels to hold the gate of his car
> for only forty minutes.

Perhaps the inevitable stresses and strains of travel were behind:

> TP was mildly embarrassed by our presence because,
> having slipped behind some boxes for a leak,
> he had greatly beshitten his naked bum.

English sleep authority Professor Ian Oswald reported thinking as he was teetering on sleep's brink:

> Or squawns of medication allow me to ungather.

Here he managed to father two neologisms – squawns and ungather – in one go. Fortunately, dream analysts don't seem to have tried to focus their gaze on these nonsensical hypnagogic scraps. Sometimes the fantastic phrases are accompanied by sharp body movements known as hypnic jerks, the sudden twitch of an arm or leg. The near-sleeper can grip conscious thought again with these jerks, or sometimes not be aware of them. Ofen they give a bit of a fright to the bed partner.

Some people can have these arcane sleep-onset experiences during the day, out of the mental blancmange of daydreaming arising some tart, if strictly meaningless, image. One such is provided by Chris Wallace-Crabbe in what he calls a 'morning mini-dream' he had after he'd arrived in Rome. 'I saw a man handling tangled rope,' he says, 'and either heard or spoke the Kraus-like utterance:

> He who ties a knot around his thumb has
> other knots up his sleeve for himself.'

It might seem logical that at night we would slide from these hypnagogic episodes into full-blown dreaming sleep, that these samples were merely precursors. But it doesn't happen that way. The first period of sleep is non-REM, in which dreaming, while possible, is unlikely. The first REM, or dreaming, sleep doesn't usually happen until between seventy and ninety minutes after sleep begins, and then it is brief, lasting maybe only five minutes. The next chapter of REM sleep is usually about three hours into the sleep and lasts about ten minutes. As we go into and out of REM and non-REM during the night, the average dream episode is quarter of an hour, but there's no firm rule, and the transition from one sleep type to the other is not abrupt. Although people like to talk about sleeping 'deeply', the term has little meaning; it's about as hard to quantify depth of sleep as it is to measure accurately human emotion. Delta waves on an electroencephalograph don't really tell us anything about quality.

Those who have dared to interpret dreams have had all sorts of scorn heaped on them. There isn't even agreement on whether or not dreams are worth wondering about. The Talmud tells Jews that each dream has a meaning (unless it is provoked by fasting), and one of the many dream interpreters in Jerusalem, Rabbi Chisda, said: 'The dream which is not interpreted is like a letter which is not read.'

Cicero put the opposite view in his poem 'On Divination': 'Dreams are not entitled to any credit or respect whatever,' he said. He went on to argue: 'If, then, dreams do not come from God, and if there are no objects in nature with which they have a necessary sympathy and connection, and if it is impossible by experiments and observations to arrive at a sure interpretation of them, the consequence is that dreams are not entitled to any credit or respect whatever... Let us reject, therefore, this divination of dreams, as well as all other kinds. For, to speak truly, that superstition has extended itself through all nations, and has oppressed the intellectual energies of all men, and has betrayed them into endless imbecilities.'

Freud, of course, grasped the Talmud's line. And he decided that dream interpretation, like charity, begins at home. At first he felt that he couldn't use the dreams of his patients undergoing psychoanalysis because the patients were neurotic. With some reluctance, he decided that his theories on dreams required him to expose his own. 'If I was to report on my own dreams,' he wrote, 'it inevitably followed that I should have to reveal to the public gaze more of the intimacies of my mental life than I liked, or than is normally necessary for any writer who is a man of science and not a poet. Such was the painful but unavoidable necessity...'

Freud's theory, at its barest, is that all dreams represent unfulfilled wishes. To those of us who would immediately come up with dreams that couldn't *possibly* represent a wish – for example a nightmare, or losing your shirt at the races – Freud's argument is that dreams often wear disguise, and frequently wishes are suppressed or repressed.

Since his death in 1939, after more than a dozen operations over many years for cancer of the mouth, Freud's reputation has always been under challenge. Yet much of what he said seems to have been misinterpreted. It is true that he can be made to contradict himself, but then you could use the eye-for-an-eye and turn-the-other-cheek discrepancy to dismiss the whole Bible.

For a start, Freud said he was against 'symbolic' dream interpretation, by which he meant a procedure that 'considers the content of the dream as a whole and seeks to replace it by another content which is intelligible and in certain respects analogous to the original one'. He said this method breaks down where dreams are both unintelligible and confused. Freud also rejected what he called the 'decoding' method, one which nevertheless has proved at least commercially successful, as you will see if you look in any big bookshop today. He disliked decoding because 'it treats dreams as a kind of cryptography in which each sign can be translated into another sign having a known meaning, in accordance with a fixed key'. Giving an example, he said: 'Suppose, for instance, that I have dreamt of a letter and also of a funeral. If I consult a "dream book", I find that "letter" must be translated by "trouble" and "funeral" by "betrothal". It then remains for me to link together the key words which I have deciphered in this way and to transpose the result into the future tense.' The problem, as he pointed out, is that 'everything depends on the trustworthiness of the "key" – the dream book – and of this we have no guarantee'.

Freud's method was to cut up dreams into little pieces and to get the subject to give associations, or background thoughts, to each piece, rather than trying to make sense out of the whole dream straight off. One of his classic examples is his interpretation of one of his own dreams about a patient called Irma, who was also a family friend. The scenario is very complicated, involving Freud's fear of misdiagnosis, professional jealousy, his problems in using cocaine on himself to treat nasal swelling, and concern about the health of his wife and one of his daughters. What struck Freud about the dream, when he had examined it, almost sentence by sentence, and had found explanations for the often weird thoughts, was that it represented wish fulfilment.

He felt this was his great breakthrough, that he had

been led into 'the full daylight of sudden discovery'. He believed enough to state: '. . . dreams are not meaningless, they are not absurd; they do not imply that one portion of our store of ideas is asleep while another portion is beginning to wake. On the contrary, they are psychical phenomena of complete validity – fulfilments of wishes; they can be inserted into the chain of intelligible waking mental acts; they are constructed by a highly complicated activity of the mind.'

Freud argued that there was no such thing as a trivial dream. 'We do not allow our sleep to be disturbed by trifles,' he declared. And he also believed that dreams, which on the surface may appear to be innocuous, are really very often steeped in hidden passion. 'The apparently innocent dreams turn out to be quite the reverse when we take the trouble to analyse them. They are, if I may say so, wolves in sheep's clothing.'

Freud knew that he was on dangerous ground here. And people queued up with dreams of stunning banality to prove him wrong. What enabled his theory to survive, at least in his own mind, was his Sherlock Holmes-like powers of detection and deduction, and his handy claim that we can distort or censor our dreams to the extent that we often produce an image that is the exact opposite of what we are really concerned about; that is, if we dream that a shop is closed, we really mean that it's open.

Freud gives an example of one such mundane dream, in which whether or not a shop is open takes on a remarkable new significance.

The dream was had by a woman whom Freud described as 'cultivated, reserved and undemonstrative in her behaviour'. This was what she reported: 'I dreamt that I arrived too late at the market and could get nothing either from the butcher or from the woman who sells vegetables.' Freud must have scratched his head a bit; this was hardly the stuff of Harold Robbins. Like the fishing fortune teller, he asked her to flesh it out just a little. The woman's more detailed account was this: 'She dreamt she was going to the market with her cook, who was carrying a basket. After she had asked for something, the butcher said to her, "That's not obtainable any longer", and offered her something else, adding, "This is good, too." She rejected it and went on to the woman who sells vegetables, who tried to get her to buy a peculiar vegetable that was tied up in bundles but was of a black colour. She said, "I don't recognize that; I won't take it."'

Freud set to work. He established straight away that the dream did have what modern analysts call 'day residue', or a connection to real events in waking life during the preceding day or two. The woman *had* gone to the market, she *had* been too late to buy anything. Freud said: 'The sitution seemed to shape itself into the phrase *Die Fleischbank war schon geschlossen* (the meat shop was closed).'

In a flash, as it were, Freud had found the key to the dream. The woman may have really meant the opposite to what she had said. Deep down she'd meant *Du hast deine Fleischbank offen*, or 'your meat shop's open', which is Viennese slang for 'Your fly is undone'.

Freud admitted at this stage, however, that the woman had not actually used the words about the meat shop being closed/open. So he examined the dream report more carefully, probing as he went. Here he worked on another of his beliefs, which was that direct speech in a dream is derived from something that has been actually spoken in real life, although the scheming dreaming psyche may delete words or take them out of context.

He started with the butcher's remark, 'That's not

obtainable any longer.' Here the connection to be made
was Freud himself. 'A few days earlier,' he says, 'I had
explained to the patient that the earliest experiences of
childhood were "not obtainable any longer" as such, but
were replaced in analysis by "transferences" and dreams.
So *I* was the butcher and she was rejecting these
transferences into the present of old habits of thinking
and feeling.'

The next thread was the woman's remark in the dream,
'I don't recognize that; I won't take it.' Freud decided that
the phrase had to be divided up. It emerged that this was
something she had said the day before to her cook. The
two had had a row, and the woman had added after, 'I
don't recognize that', three words that she'd suppressed
in her dream: 'Behave yourself properly!' Freud felt that
he'd made another breakthrough because these words
'would have been the appropriate words to use if someone had ventured to make improper suggestions and had
forgotten to "close his meat shop".'

To cut a long interpretation short, Freud went on to
work out that the bundled up vegetables the woman did
not recognize and would not take were asparagus and
black radishes, and as he points out, 'No knowledgeable
person of either sex will ask for an interpretation of
asparagus.' He ends the analysis frustratingly by saying:
'We need not enquire now into the full meaning of the
dream. So much is quite clear: it *had* a meaning and that
meaning was far from innocent.

To put us out of our misery, however, Freud added a
footnote to explain that 'the dream concealed a phantasy
of my behaving in an improper and sexually provocative
manner, and of the patient putting up a defence against
my conduct'. Of course, Freud didn't really have his 'meat
shop open'; the dream was just a manifestation of a

trauma that went way back to his patient's early life.

Freud has been attacked for tracing all dreams back to sex, but this, too, is unfair. Certainly he argued that anxiety dreams usually have a sexual springboard, but he flatly denied that he'd ever maintained that *every* dream was sexual. In 1925, twenty-five years after *The Interpretation of Dreams* was published, Freud wrote that this widespread belief showed 'the unconscientious manner in which critics are accustomed to perform their functions, and the readiness with which opponents overlook the clearest statements if they do not give scope to their aggressive inclinations'. He cited as evidence the fact that he had interpreted a lot of his own children's dreams and that, while all were based on wish fulfilment, they had no sexual connotation. Among them were his kids' wanting to be taken sailing on a lake, to go climbing, dreams of hunger and thirst.

It is hard not to feel some sympathy for Freud. Like most who upset the status quo, he was often mocked or ignored in his own time, and he's been sniped at ever since. He's said to have endured the long slow ravage of cancer inside his mouth and nasal cavity with great stoicism before his death in England in 1939, having fled Vienna a year earlier when Hitler invaded Austria. Right or wrong, he was certainly a great thinker, and he probably did more for the world by giving it psychoanalysis than he would have had he not made a last-minute decision when he went to university to switch to medicine from law. Had he left both alone, he would have made a superb writer of whodunnits.

It was partly his views on sex that ended the friendship between Freud and that other doyen of dream interpretation, Carl Gustav Jung of Switzerland. Jung, who died in 1961, was for a long time the heir apparent to Freud, but in the end he described Freud as a great but tragic man.

Jung's approach to dream interpretation, after he had parted from Freud, was more mystical, less cut and dried, full of shadow and myth. He wrote, in his eighty-third year: '. . . what man appears to be can only be expressed by way of myth. Myth is more individual and expresses life more precisely than does science. Science works with concepts of averages which are far too general to do justice to the subjective variety of an individual life.'

Jung, however, did go along with Freud for a considerable time, a fact that may be not unrelated to his very first dream being about a giant, one-eyed phallus in an underground cave. The dream so troubled Jung that he didn't mention it to a soul until he was sixty-five years old. No doubt the clergyman's son also refrained from telling many people about one of his most memorable dreams when he was a schoolboy. It concerned the beautiful cathedral in Basel, near which the Jungs lived.

Young Carl was an extremely thoughtful, yet dreamy young man, his head filled with conceptual questions most modern kids wouldn't entertain for a minute. He was very good at schoolwork, but soon realized that life was a lot easier if you came second in your class rather than top. On the few occasions when he pulled out all stops and wrote a brilliant critical essay, his teachers accused him of plagiarism.

Jung's cathedral dream came when he was going through a stretch of mental agony, unsure about himself, trying desperately to comprehend God and the devil. In waking life the cathedral stood tall in his mind, yet he sensed that he'd been avoiding a certain dream. At last he let it happen. 'I gathered all my courage, as though I were about to leap forthwith into hell-fire, and let the thought come. I saw before me the cathedral, the blue sky. God sits on His golden throne, high above the world – and from under the throne an enormous turd falls upon the sparkling new roof, shatters it, and breaks the walls of the cathedral asunder.'

This dream is not recounted here to mock Jung's scholarly reputation, but to show that kings and academics dream in the same basic and graphic language as does the common man. As it happened, this dream had great significance for Jung, who interpreted it as showing that God stood 'omnipotent and free, above His Bible and His Church'. Perhaps because he had trouble grasping his father's faith, Jung saw the effects of a turd dropped from a great height as a statement that 'God refuses to abide by traditions, no matter how sacred.' After the dream Jung felt 'an enormous, an indescribable relief'! He said: '. . . grace had come upon me, and with it an unutterable bliss such as I had never known. I wept for happiness and gratitude.' Later he found some link and consolation in Job (9: 30-31): 'Though I wash myself with snow water . . . yet shalt thou plunge me in the mire.'

Jung was twenty-five when Freud's *Interpretation of Dreams* was first published, and the young psychiatrist discovered that 'it linked up with my own ideas'. This was not necessarily a pleasant realization because Freud was *persona non grata* in the academic world. Nevertheless, Jung became a follower. Even at this early stage, however, he didn't believe that all neuroses were caused by sexual repression or trauma.

The two men first met in Vienna in February 1907, Jung recalling later that it was 1 pm and that they talked almost non-stop for thirteen hours. The young Swiss was a bit over-awed and felt unable to take on Freud in debate, but Jung's spiritual nature was already beginning to rebel. 'Above all, Freud's attitude towards the spirit seemed to me highly questionable,' he wrote. 'Wherever in a person or a work of art, an expression of spirituality (in the intellectual, not the supernatural sense) came to light, he suspected it, and insinuated that it was repressed sexuality.' Jung felt that on this basis the whole of culture would be 'a mere farce, the morbid consequence of repressed sexuality'. Jung says that Freud's reply to him was: 'Yes, so it is, and that is just a curse of fate against which we are powerless to contend.'

Jung claimed that when Freud spoke of his sexual theory, 'his tone became urgent, almost anxious, and all signs of his critical and sceptical manner vanished. A strange, deeply moved expression came over his face'. Jung, in his eighties, said he could still recall vividly Freud saying to him: 'My dear Jung, promise me never to abandon the sexual theory. That is the most essential thing of all. You see, we must make a dogma of it, an unshakeable bulwark.'

The sight of two psychiatrists contradicting each other on an issue of the psyche can strain sanity, as those who have watched court proceedings will know. The split between Freud and Jung, while not quite so public, was torrid, Freud clinging to his theory like a lifebuoy, Jung ascending the heights of spirituality and mysticism. Jung described the tension between them when he visited Freud in Vienna in 1909. He said that while Freud was talking he felt a curious sensation. 'It was as if my diaphragm were made of iron and were becoming red-hot – a glowing vault.' At that moment there was a loud cracking noise from the bookcase next to them in the room, startling both men. Jung says: 'I said to Freud: "There, that is an example of a so-called catalytic exteriorization phenomenon."' Freud dismissed the suggestion that there was any connection between Jung's belly and the bookcase as 'sheer bosh'. But Jung said defiantly: 'It is not. You are mistaken, Herr Professor. And to prove my point I now predict that in a moment there will be another loud report!' This was a fairly risky gambit, but, as Jung tells the story: 'Sure enough, no sooner had I said the words than the same detonation went off in the bookcase. To this day I do not know what gave me this certainty. But I knew beyond all doubt that the report would come again. Freud only stared aghast at me.'

For his part, Freud said in a letter to Jung about the incident that it could be explained by creaking oak boards, adding that the noises had happened again may times after Jung had left the house, 'yet never in connection with my thoughts and never when I was considering you or your special problem'. Assuming his paternal role towards Jung, he wrote: 'The furniture stands before me spiritless and dead, like nature silent and godless before the poet after the passing of the gods of Greece.'

Now all this may seem to be idle digression, but the battle between Freud and Jung did not really finish with their deaths; modern dream interpreters still tend to lean for or against one of these two pillars, as you will find if you go to seminars on the subject. So, before giving you some sample dreams from twentieth-century Australians, let's follow Freud and Jung a little further towards their crossroads.

The denouement came when the two men were travelling together to America by ship in 1909, passing the hours trying to interpret each other's dreams. According to Jung, Freud wasn't able to make anything of some of his dreams, although he was not critical of him for this because not even the best analyst can be expected to unravel every riddle. The end came, however, when Jung was trying to decipher one of Freud's (in deference to Freud he didn't reveal 'the problem' Freud's dream involved). He asked Freud for some more details of his private life so that he could make a better interpretation.

Upon this request, according to Jung's version of events, Freud reacted with a look 'of the utmost suspicion', and replied, 'But I cannot risk my authority!' That statement burned itself into Jung's memory.

But worse was to come. During the voyage, Jung had one of the most significant dreams in his life, yet when Freud tried to interpret it Jung lied to him about it. In the dream Jung found himself in a house, a two-storey one, which, even though he didn't know much about the place, was his own. When the dream began he was in the upper storey, which was expensively furnished. Realizing that he didn't know what the place was like below, he went downstairs. Here it was darker, and the building seemed much older, as though from mediaeval times. Strolling about, Jung opened a door to discover a stone staircase to a cellar. It was a beautiful, vaulted cellar, again much older, perhaps dating from Roman times, he thought. He looked down to see a stone slab with a ring in it. Lifting the slab he revealed another narrow stone staircase descending still further. This took him to a cave cut into rock, and on its dusty floor were two human skulls, almost disintegrated. Then he woke up.

Jung said that Freud's main interest was in the two skulls, to which he returned repeatedly as he tried to interpret the dream. Jung was caught here. Already in his own mind he felt he had an inkling of the meaning of his dream, but he wasn't confident enough to argue it against Freud. At the same time, he knew full well what Freud's harping on the skulls was aimed at – a death wish. 'He returned to them repeatedly, and urged me to find a wish in connection with them,' said Jung. 'What did I think about these skulls, and whose were they? I knew perfectly well, of course, what he was driving at.' So he caved in and told Freud: 'My wife and sister-in-law.' Jung, newly married at the time, had no such wish, and he was aware that his conduct was not above reproach, but he claimed that Freud seemed greatly relieved by his answer. Jung's reverence for Freud was hereafter dented irreparably. 'I saw from this that he was completely helpless in dealing with certain kinds of dreams and had to take refuge in his doctrine.'

So what did Jung's house mean, given that it was not based on a secret wish to do away with his wife and her sister? Jung interpreted the house as his own psyche, with the second-storey room representing his consciousness. 'The ground floor stood for the first level of the unconscious. The deeper I went, the more alien and the darker the scene became,' he said. 'In the cave I discovered the remains of a primitive culture, that is, the world of primitive man within myself – a world which can scarcely be reached or illuminated by consciousness. The primitive psyche of man borders on the life of the animal soul, just as the caves of prehistoric times were usually inhabited by animals before men laid claim to them.' This dream not only made permanent the breach between Freud and Jung but also provided the basis for Jung's enduring theory of archetypes.

In the end, Freud and Jung grew wider apart. Jung could not go along with Freud's theories on dream distortion any more than he could accept the imperative of wish fulfilment. 'I was never able to agree with Freud that the dream is a "facade" behind which its meaning lies hidden – a meaning already known but maliciously, so to speak, withheld from consciousness,' Jung wrote late in his life.

'To me dreams are part of nature, which harbours no intention to deceive, but expresses something as best it can. These forms of life, too, have no wish to deceive our eyes, but we may deceive ourselves because our eyes are shortsighted . . . Long before I met Freud I regarded the unconscious, and dreams, which are its direct exponents, as natural processes to which no arbitrariness can be attributed, and above all no legerdemain.'

For the rest of his life Jung was on a quest. 'My whole being was seeking for something still unknown which might confer meaning upon the banality of life.' More than a quarter of a century after his death, the search for such a miracle was continuing. And in 1983 came the devastating suggestion, from a Nobel prizewinner, that the dreaming that Jung, Freud and many great thinkers before them had agonized over was a load of old rubbish. Dr Francis Crick, an Englishman who got the Nobel for his work in unravelling the structure of DNA, and Graeme Mitchison, of the Salk Institute in California, proposed that the function of sleep and dreaming was merely an empty-out for the brain, a purging of the overloaded computer.

Francis Crick and Graeme Mitchison argued that impulses received by the brain could feed back on themselves, giving unwanted or undesirable 'modes of mutual excitation'. They wrote: 'We propose that such undesirable modes are detected and suppressed by a special mechanism which operates during REM sleep and is, loosely speaking, the opposite of learning.' They called this 'reverse learning' or 'unlearning'.

Explaining the interrelationships between the brain's neurons, axons and synapses, the two come up with the theory that within our heads something is necessary to 'damp down' the system, perhaps a bit the way a fuse

wire can avert trouble when too much electricity is
pumping into the house. 'Put more simply,' they say, after
a long explanation, 'we suggest that in REM sleep we
unlearn our unconscious dreams. We dream in order to
forget.' Admittedly they are only postulating, but Freud
and Jung would be having nightmares in their graves to
hear: 'In our view of REM sleep, trying to remember one's
dreams should perhaps not be encouraged, because such
remembering may help to retain patterns of thought
which are better forgotten. These are the very patterns the
organism was trying to damp down.'

This 'rubbish bin' theory of dreams was not new, but no
one last century had the neurological knowledge they
were able to use to bolster their argument. Freud did
anticipate that such an argument would grow and gather
strength. His argument against the theory was that our
dreams are frequently filled with images from childhood.
If dreams were meant to clean the slate, he said, 'we could
only conclude that dreams perform their function most
inadequately'.

Whether dreaming is merely 'ten fingers of a man who
knows nothing of music wandering over the keys of a
piano' or is 'the royal road to the unconscious' may never
be proved either way. But there is no doubt that many
people spend a lot of time noting down, pondering and
trying to make some sense of their dreams. And many
claim that they have received great flashes of inspiration
or answers to problems from their sleeping heads. This
has always been so. Robert Louis Stevenson was scratch-
ing around for a plot, couldn't think of a thing, when he
slept and dreamt of the characters who became Dr Jekyll
and Mr Hyde. One of the great breakthroughs of organic
chemistry came to the German Friedrich Kekulé during a
dream in which he saw six snakes biting each other's tails

and spinning around in a circle. He'd hit upon the structure of the benzene molecule. They are just two of the many from the world of arts and science who have found their inspiration in dreaming. Lesser mortals claim to have discovered more mundane answers, such as whether or not to buy a certain house or car, whether to shoot the dog.

Proving such claims is naturally difficult, although it has been tried at various times. William Dement's Stanford sleep centre in California tried giving 500 undergraduate students problems to solve in their sleep. The idea was that they were to look at the problem fifteen minutes before going to bed. In the morning they had to write down any dream they could recall from the night, then, if the problem hadn't been solved, to spend another fifteen minutes on it. The three problems, tackled on successive nights, were those infuriating sequential brainteasers you find in quiz books. One, for example, was to name the next two letters in this sequence: O,T,T,F,F. The clues given were that the sequence is infinite, and that the rule for finding any letter in the chain is simple. For those interested in testing the theory of dream inspiration themselves, don't read on, sleep on it. I tried this myself, but must confess to having woken up with nothing more inspiring than a blank, rather irritable mind and a dry mouth. The answer is that the next two letters in the sequence are S, S. The letters represent the first in counting from nought to infinity, One, Two, Three, Four, Five, Six, Seven in this sample.

With a complex scoring system, the Stanford experimenters assessed a total of 1,148 attempts to solve such problems while asleep. The result was that eighty-seven dreams could be related to a problem, either directly or indirectly, but there were only nine correct solutions, and two of these the students had arrived at in the fifteen-minute pre-sleep reading. One of the dream solutions – to the sequence example explained above – came to a student this way: 'I was standing in an art gallery looking at the paintings on the wall. As I walked down the hall, I began to count the paintings – one, two, three, four, five. But as I came to the sixth and seventh, the paintings had been ripped from their frames! I stared at the empty frames with a peculiar feeling that some mystery was about to be solved. Suddenly I realized that the sixth and seventh spaces were the solution to the problem!'

Obviously instant problem-solving is a big demand on any dreamer. The great breakthrough dreams such as Kekulé's came after long periods of waking agonizing. With artistic dream inspiration it is even harder to measure dream influence because the capturing – the writing down or painting – is obviously done afterwards in waking life, when the conscious is back on deck and interfering, censoring and upgrading. Many poets, myself included, do claim to have had whole chunks come to them in their sleep. The English writer A. C. Benson woke up in the middle of the night and scratched down on a scrap of bedside paper all of a poem called 'The Phoenix': 'It came to me so apparently without any definite volition of my own that I don't profess to understand or be able to interpret the symbolism,' Benson wrote.

> By feathers green, across Casbeen,
> The pilgrims track the Phoenix flown,
> By gems he strewed in waste and wood
> And jewelled plumes at random thrown.
>
> Till wandering far by moon and star,
> They stand beside the fruitful pyre,
> Whence breaking bright with sanguine light,
> The impulsive bird forgets his sire.

Those ashes shine like ruby wine,
Like bag of Tyrian murex spilt;
The claw, the jowl of the flying fowl
Are with the glorious anguish gilt.

So rare the light, so rich the sight,
Those pilgrim men, on profit bent,
Drop hands and eyes and merchandise,
And are with gazing most content.

Arthur Benson, whose father Edward was Archbiship of Canterbury, was a scholarly man who taught at Eton. He said of 'The Phoenix' that he'd 'never had a similar experience before or since' and added: 'I can really offer no explanation either of the idea of the poem or its interpretation.' Benson, who died in 1925, has not been ranked among the top echelon of British poets (he also wrote the words to the anthem 'Land of Hope and Glory'), but I think 'The Phoenix' is a fine poem, very evocative. In case you're wondering about the spilt Tyrian murex in the penultimate stanza, it's a purple dye.

My own experience of dream-manufactured poetry came in 1985, when this book was in gestation and I was also publishing an anthology of my own poetry – entitled *Above Water*. A close friend of mine, an artist called John Druce, was to illustrate some of the poems. I spend a lot of time at the Druces' place, in the Victorian seaside town of Barwon Heads. The old house was built by John's father, a fisherman, and the garden is old and established. The other relevant factor is that I very rarely recall my dreams. I must be one of those people who regularly resurface during non-REM sleep. Like Arthur Benson, never before or since have I dreamt a poem. But this one came to me, virtually word for word, as I dreamt, and was clearly printed in my head when I awoke, for some reason, about 2 am one day.

Profligate with jewellery she stands,
Dripping wealth.
Even her aged, wrinkly arms
Are loaded.
At the throat, the best gems
Gloat their richness to passing eyes
That lust.
Lips are licked involuntarily.

Bedazzled uninvite,
I rip and bite one full ruby stone
From near the heart.
Shattering,
A delight of sharp slivers
Lacerates taste buds;
Light cascades pricelessly
Down my chin.

What dividends!
Such pregnancy!
Druces' 24-carat
Apple tree.

The Druces do have a very old, lichen-covered apple tree
in their garden, one that despite its age produces delicious
apples every year. I wrote the poem on a piece of paper
beside the bed and, after lying there wondering for quite
some time, went back to sleep. When I woke again, I
quickly reached for the paper to ensure that the dream
inspiration wasn't itself a dream. I included it in the
anthology because it came, as it were, from a different
source from the other poems.

Many of the letters I received when I asked for people to
write to me about their sleep and their dreams included
dream-inspired poems. The one that I liked best came
from Dorothy Simmons, a thirty-five-year-old secondary

school teacher who lives at Albury on the Victoria-New
South Wales border. She says: 'I think that part of my
fascination with dreams is that through them I may gain
access to such smidgins of originality as I possess, which
otherwise seem to have great difficulty in getting themselves delivered into conscious expression . . . The imag-
ing process of the subconscious seems to me directly
parallel to the poetic. Perhaps there is a similar function in
sensitizing us to the atmosphere of truth. That phrase
sounds pretentious, particularly when you think of the
possibility that the subconscious is just the garbage tip of
the brain. I don't, but even if I did, I'd still want to
scavenge. You never know what you might find!' Dorothy
Simmons's poem is called 'T. Rex, Gent.' (She explained
that Gent is just that, a contraction of gentleman.):

Up from the sanded, C-scooped shore
Minced
The dinosaurs
In the endearing diminutive of distance,
They seemed elegant, effete:
Slope-shouldered Victorians
With drooping, ineffectual hands.
T. Rex, Gent . . .
Not Tyrannosaurus.
We watched from the glass rectangle
In which the whole world was contained.
As the sand turned to gravel,
As the dinosaur steps scraped closer,
Churning the grit.
Now the hands hang like eagles,
For swooping, for tearing . . .
And the door creaks away from us
And our eyes turn to that other eye
Covered . . . uncovered . . . covered

By a scaly lid.
Convex sheen of a reptilian eye,
Cold and unavoidable as radar.
TYRANNOSAURUS
Clammy. Cold. Blood-crusty scales.
And the girl outside, outside,
In the pink angora jumper,
How her face zooms in and out,
Screaming, screaming . . .

To many people the powerful imagery of dreams comes in prose, and concerns more humdrum day-to-day matters. But when you have read a lot of dream reports you realize that nearly all the driving human emotions are there somewhere – power, fear, love, insecurity and sexuality.

A more down-to-earth report came from 'Mrs Gwen W', who lives in the Melbourne suburb of East Brighton. She says: 'For a few years now I have recorded some of my dreams and have found them very helpful in (a) knowing oneself better (b) getting direction, and (c) confirming decisions, etc.' 'Gwen W' provides two sample dreams, with her own interpretations.

'I was with my husband in a chemist shop. The chemist was giving me some medicine that I had to take. I objected to this as I told him I was not on tablets for anything wrong with me. As he handed them to me, I noticed the name on the bottle was a strange name, not mine at all. The chemist could hardly believe that he had made a mistake, and re-read it and apologized. Just at this moment, his dog and my dog (I do not have a dog) started to snarl at each other. I tried to send my dog out of the shop and the chemist apologized, saying his dog is usually quiet and never does that.

'*Interpretation:* The house we were thinking of buying did not have my name on it. I had said it would be good

medicine for us to have a new home, as we are retired –
hence chemist. Dogs snapping at each other? We had got
to the stage of snapping at each other and the family,
especially over moving, and usually we are a very quiet
family. I thought this could be a confirmation dream as we
had decided before going to bed and having the dream not
to buy the house.'

'Gwen W's' second dream is fascinating in that it
shows, at least in her mind, that bizarre circumstances
thrown up in sleep can have the most basic and practical
implications when translated to waking life. This is how
she explained it:

'I was in a room and a Catholic priest entered. I
immediately ran to him and embraced him, kissed him,
and he responded as if I knew him well. While this was
happening, out of the wardrobe stepped a man. He
approached us and condemned what we were doing. I felt
embarrassed but immediately justified our actions by
saying we were going to be married and the priest was
leaving the church. The man accepted this solemnly and
faded into the background.

'*Interpretation:* I had asked myself for a dream as we
were about to invest money in Telecom, and I was not
looking forward to telling our bank manager that we
would not be reinvesting the money that matured in two
weeks with his bank. I felt he would disapprove and
condemn Telecom. The priest was a Catholic and not
Protestant (I am Protestant), but this made me think of my
brother-in-law, who is Catholic – and works at Telecom.
Therefore I knew it was about Telecom that the dream
was referring. Also the marriage was a contract, and this
was what we were entering into. The man in the wardrobe
was the bank manager whom I thought would not
approve. I stood up to him in the dream, and he faded

away. This gave me confidence to face up to him when we made the changeover.

'This dream again assured us that what we were about to do would be okay because we had a lot of doubts at the time. The investment was highly successful.'

Freud, Jung or any of the thousands of modern-day dream-analysing psychologists might have come up with entirely different interpretations. But the important thing is that 'Gwen W' is satisfied with what she is getting, her own analysis is clearly a useful tool in her life.

Melbourne psychologist Doris Brett, who is attached to one of the big teaching hospitals and who gives lectures on dreaming, goes along with this. 'I think it is really important to understand that the only person who can really ratify a dream and say, "Yes, that's the right interpretation", is the dreamer him or herself. It's your dream, it's your truth. Someone can come up with the fanciest interpretation that sounds wonderful, but if it doesn't ring true to you then there's not much good in it. Obviously we can try to delude ourselves.'

Dr Brett goes along with those who believe that dreams are messages to us. 'It is important to be aware that the language of dreams is a language all its own. It's not the same as everyday English. It doesn't make sense in the normal, logical processes of our thinking. It is a rather special language, and you do need to think in that language in order to interpret the dream. It is a little bit like learning French. You wouldn't get far in France if you didn't know any French at all. Like any language, however, it is learnable; you can pick it up. It is also not like French in the sense that French is a set language; you can get a dictionary of French words and their English equivalents and the meanings will always be the same. Dream language isn't like that; there aren't any universal

symbols. Jung was very keen on the idea of universal
symbols; he talked about archetypes that appear in
dreams, such as the archetype perfect man and perfect
woman, a symbol of our ideals. He talked about the dark
shadow that we harbour, that we're scared of or threat-
ened by or have learned to repress. Certainly those sorts
of images are pretty universal, but they're not always
going to be the same for different people.

'Jung felt that what we were dealing with in dreams was
a sort of racial consciousness where the same symbols
tended to mean the same thing. I don't go along with that
because I think symbols can mean very different things to
different people. A snake, for instance, can mean something evil, dangerous, threatening. It can mean something
healing, something sly and it can mean something rather
nice if you happen to have a snake as a pet. Of course,
they can also be sexual symbols, phallic. They can be lots
of other things, depending entirely on the dreamer.'

For Doris Brett, one of the most important functions of
dreams is their way of telling us how we see ourselves.
'We see ourselves in all sorts of different ways. In some
dreams we may be on the outside, a very impassive,
uninvolved observer. That can be a very useful thing.
That dream may be telling us that we are not really getting
involved with our lives. It may be telling us that we've
been blocked from doing or feeling something. It may be
allowing us to see a situation through someone else's
eyes. Being on the outside looking in we may see a
different aspect to a situation than when we're in the
middle, where sometimes you can't see the forest for the
trees.

'We can feel in our dreams as if we're dreaming, or as if
we're young or old, stupid or clever. We can feel in charge
or out of control, happy or sad; the list is endless. The way

we see ourselves physically can also vary tremendously. If we see ourselves as very thin that dream may be telling us that we're not carrying enough weight in a given situation. We can feel very obese; maybe that's something to do with a feeling that we are being stretched out of shape. Obviously there are myriads of interpretations, and they all depend on what's happening in the rest of the dream and what's happening in the dreamer's life.'

She points out that we do not always look like ourselves in our dreams. 'Sometimes we can be dreaming of a dog coming into the room, and we are the dog.' Doris Brett says a good place to start interpreting is to ask yourself: 'What was I doing, what was I thinking, what was I feeling?' 'The next thing you might ask,' she says, is "How am I seeing or experiencing the other people/objects/animals in my dream? Who are they? What are they doing? How am I relating to them and them to me?" They don't have to be whos, they can be whats: houses, cars, horses.

'Another thing dreams tell us about is how we see our impulses. For instance, if we are driving a car, this can contain messages about our impulses and drives in the world. Are we driving the car, or are we being driven? Is someone taking us for a ride? Is someone taking care of us? Is someone driving recklessly? Are we scared in the passenger seat? Are we impatient that we're going too slowly? Are we worried because we have taken the wrong turning? Do we *know* whether we have taken the wrong or right turning? If we are driving the car, are we driving well or badly? Is the car responding to our guidance on the steering wheel, or the accelerator? It is a good car, a safe car, a bad car? These will all go to tell us how we are experiencing our impulses, needs and drives in the real world.'

An example of such a car dream came to me from a Victorian woman, like Dorothy Simmons also a secondary schoolteacher. 'Angela O' says: 'For many years I have had a recurring dream that I am driving a car without a licence (I did do that once when I was nineteen. I am now thirty-nine and a law-abiding teacher). Last year I was asked to act as head of the humanities department at my school. Because of problems in the department, the then head was leaving. I dreamed that I was called out to drive an old battered ute. I climbed in and noticed a long crack down the dashboard (on the left-hand side of the car – the steering wheel was on the left, too) from which petrol was leaking. I started the ute, and it immediatley ran quickly backwards down a hill.

'A few weeks later I dreamt that I was parking in an underground car park and I banged into a car. That car then hit another, and so on. Every car in the park was badly damaged.

'At the end of last year, I gained a promotion which confirmed my position as head of department. I was then asked if I would be acting vice-principal during second term. I dreamt that I was driving a huge semi-trailer. I swerved when going around a corner and knocked over two white posts. Yes, I can think of two people who might have been acting vice-principal.'

'Angela O' says that driving has always been significant in her life. When we first corresponded she'd had her licence only six months because before that she had lacked the confidence to go for it. 'I believed that driving would be too difficult for me,' she said. In a later letter she said: 'Since I last wrote I have had two more driving dreams. In one I drove a big fast car through a whole lot of pedestrians. In another, I had left my husband and children in our Land Cruiser and I was riding a bicycle. I found the journey frightening and was very pleased to get back to the safety of the big vehicle. I have been acting vice-principal for three weeks now and, as you can deduce, some days go much better than others.'

What most surprised me in all my correspondence with dreamers was how frank they were prepared to be. Also, as a rule, most people were able to come up with some interpretation of their own if I asked them to. One quirky aspect, which I don't quite understand, is that some people's handwriting changed dramatically during our correspondence. This may happen in any correspondence for all I know, or it may be a manifestation of problems of identity among vivid dreamers. Many of the dreams had fairly explicit sexual content. For this reason the following dream and explanation from an eighteen-year-old Victorian girl has had the names and place names changed. The dreamer, 'Sally J' first provides some background:

'I have just spent three days at some friends' new house – they are Sue and Deidre. Deidre has been my closest friend for three and a half years now. She is having an affair with her first serious boyfriend – she is seventeen, he twenty-seven. He lives in Bendigo. She draws attention to their relationship to me occasionally as she is quite proud of this new adult status she considers herself to have acquired. I only know her boyfriend vaguely and had decided I did not like him. Then Sue told me privately how lucky Deidre was as he is considerate, intelligent, an "all-rounder" and is never in the way when he stays with them. My mother commented yesterday on hearing this that Deidre had got "a good man".

'Last night I had the following dream: Deidre and her boyfriend were planning driving to Melbourne. He had a long chat with me, and we got along extremely well. While Deidre was busying herself arranging the trip, I sat

on his knee, and he very tenderly caressed me. I was
surprised and flattered, but did not respond. Deidre also
looked at us, also surprised, slightly amused, and not at all
upset. I thought to myself, Well, it is all right as long as she
doesn't mind. It obviously means nothing to me, although
he does seem very keen. I also thought, Perhaps she sees
it as his way of trying to win me over. Her boyfriend and I
had sex, which I enjoyed, and I was rather pleased that
Deidre knew that I could do what she was doing; I also
enjoyed testing her to see if she would be jealous.

'Then the dream changed, or rather I changed the
dream, so that I slept with another boy, Deidre's brother,
who I am in reality very attracted to, although he dislikes
me. In this partnership I was responsive, proud of myself
and more comfortable, as, knowing him very well, I
continue to feel committed to him.'

The morning after this dream 'Sally J' tried to interpret
its meaning. She came up with three possibilities. '(a) I am
jealous of Deidre and feel left behind, and was trying to
get back at her for hurt feelings, (b) I still do not trust her
boyfriend, my dream being proof that he had merely won
over Sue, as he could me, and he would not be faithful to
Deidre, or (c) my revenge on Deidre's brother for rejecting
me. All three components could be present in my dream.'

After much thought, 'Sally J' said in a later letter, 'I've
come to the conclusion that I was probably jealous.' But
she adds: 'I also often follow in my dreams the logical
conclusion of what has happened – often a conclusion
that is hurtful and perhaps shocking to me – to see how I
cope. It is a device of "playing out" my worst fears so if
they *do* occur in reality I won't be surprised and can
remain composed. I think this is the motivation for the
dream.'

'Sally J' had the advantage in her dream of not having

to decipher symbols. She did have to seek answers for certain situations and events, but the people were real, and there was nothing fantastic to unravel, no weird images and juxtapositions.

One dreamer from Tasmania sent me a swag of dreams in which she flies, pictures turn into peanut butter sandwiches and she is able to walk through glass. One of the most amusing sent by Beris Reid, of Kings Meadows, Tasmania, went like this:

'Awoke from my dream laughing. I had been walking along with a jolly group. I was wearing a kilt. The chap behind me placed both his hands on my hips and grasped my skirt and held on – so that I actually walked out of the skirt. At that moment a Japanese man in a tunic affair leapt to my left side brandishing his samurai sword. He actually thought he had whipped off my skirt with his blade. He looked at my pantyhose-clad legs, then back at his sword (which, incidentally, was only a handle with no blade in evidence) with such an amazed expression on his face that I burst out laughing, and of course woke myself up.'

Beris Reid doesn't venture an interpretation, but you can almost make a party game out of guessing what, if anything, her subconscious was playing at. Or it may not have been playful at all; it may have some deep and important meaning.

Many people do conjure up highly amusing symbols in their dreams. Psychologist Doris Brett, again on dream language: 'The language is very much a pictorial one. It often runs along the lines of metaphors and puns, plays on words. It condenses several thoughts and ideas into one and uses popular idiomatic language that's very metaphorical. If you've got a friend, for instance, whom you think of as a good friend, and you have a dream in which he or she is crawling like a snake in some long grass, the dream may be telling you that your friend *is* in fact a snake in the grass, that underneath the friendly, helpful exterior is something more nasty. We can dream of living next door to a bird that has honey on its beak; that may be our dream language telling us that we're living next door to a sticky beak. You find these sorts of beautiful, humorous images, and they're very elegant at the same time because they really do condense many things.'

Dr Brett provides a few of the more amusing examples, although she stresses again that dreams are very personal, and images mean different things to different people. 'You can, for instance, dream about someone who is a rather matronly figure and who is standing in a courtroom wearing a wig. That's right: mother-in-law. Or you can dream about Bob Hope, and he may be symbolizing hope. Nothing to do with the real Bob Hope, but his name may simply be a play on words. In one of her books Ann Faraday (a leading British researcher) cites a dream that someone she worked with had, an absolutely gorgeous image of Bob Hope jumping down the street on a pogo stick. The message? Hope springs eternal.'

Dr Brett always gets a good laugh from audiences with that one, as she does with the image of a bunch of roses. 'This,' she says with a smile, 'can symbolize passionate love. Equally the roses can symbolize life as it is explained on the greeting card which says, "Life is a bed of roses, but you'd better watch out for the pricks."'

Doris Brett is a poet as well as a psychologist, and one of her own dreams is an example of making sense of symbols. It also illustrates the point that Freud and others made, that 'day residue', or a recent real event in your life, is often used to provide the structure for the imagery. The background to Dr Brett's dream was that she was concerned about how she had been managing her time, fitting in all the demands on it. She felt that she had been neglecting her creative writing for other writing work as a professional; the former was poetry, the latter more lucrative. The problem had been highlighted for her on the day of the dream when she learned that she had won the Anne Elder award for a first book of poetry, a huge thrill. She explains the dream:

'I was at this lovely banquet with Einstein – you may as well pick big when you choose your dinner guests in dreams – and he was old and white-haired. The banquet tables held tons and tons of different dishes and, being the pig that I am, I wanted to have everything. I was busy starting to help myself when Einstein reached out and stopped me. He said that I could eat dishes that had white things in them, but where there were green things such as peas and beans, he said, "No, you can't have those." That's all the dream was.'

When Doris Brett woke up she knew that her dream had something to do with the events of the previous day, and meaning started to fall into place very quickly. First, she knew what the banquet meant. 'When I'd heard that I'd won the prize, I'd been invited to a banquet where it was going to be presented. That explains the setting. Einstein? I think everyone's reaction to him is that he's someone very clever and wise. But he was more than that in my dream, and this I thought was just lovely. When I thought about him being old and white-haired my immediate response was to think of an elder of the tribe, and the award I'd won was the Anne Elder award. An obvious pun. What Einstein was telling me was that I had to stick to the right course, that I also mustn't put too much on my plate at once. What's more, I had to stick to the white stuff, not the green. Green is something commonly associated with greenbacks, fifthy lucre, etc. So he was saying stay away from the green stuff, stick to the white stuff. White also has significance because my book was called *The Truth About Unicorns*, which are white. Also Robert Graves wrote a book about poetry called *The White Goddess*, so I got white from him. Every single aspect of the dream has meaning, has its translation. It was a very compact dream with a very clear meaning for me, and I think remarkably elegant in the way it combined so many images. I certainly wouldn't have sat down and consciously thought it up.'

While many people determine the meaning of their dreams quite easily, a lot of people haven't a clue how to find out what their subconscious is on about. Often they will seek out a psychologist or some other self-styled analyst to help them interpret. A woman we'll call 'Jenny S' is such a case. She went to an analyst several years ago after a series of emotional crises which began after the birth of her second child – marital strife, deaths in the family, and similar difficulties. She says that she is now abe to recognize the symbolism of her dreams. 'To me they represent the internal extension of my conscious thoughts,' 'Jenny S' says. 'Of course, I am no expert and cannot be objective about my own dreams.' Here's one of them:

'I am travelling in an aeroplane over high rocky mountains and seated beside me is a faceless (male) person wearing a dark, old-fashioned suit. He has curly hair, but I can see no face, just a blank void. Suddenly the plane crashes and comes to rest on a rocky ledge. The faceless man and I are the only survivors. As we climb through the wreckage of the plane I notice that a huge fissure appears in the rocks, threatening to engulf us both.

'Something tells me that we'll need clothes and blankets to keep us warm, so I begin stuffing a pile of nappies I find down the front of my shirt. The dream ends with the two of us still standing outside the plane, waiting for something to happen.'

This dream happened when 'Jenny S's' marriage (of seven years) was very shaky, and she was having analysis. The counsellor told her that the faceless man was a part of herself waiting to be recognized, and that the crash and the rocks symbolized a drastic upheaval in her life. There was a fascinating real life sequel to the dream, as 'Jenny S' explains:

'A week after the dream I was unable to get to my regular appointment with the counsellor because I had a minor car crash on the way there (the brakes failed). I rang the counsellor in tears to tell him that I could not make the appointment. I reached into my bag to find something to dry my eyes, and found myself clutching a nappy – just like in the dream. I realized at once the similarity and was a little unnerved.'

Another of her dreams can easily be connected to her waking emotions: 'I am in a hardware shop in a small country town, and suddenly I know my lover is near me, watching me, waiting. I am frozen to the spot. I want to hide. I do not want to see him because he has told me that our relationship is over. He leaves the shop and gets into a white car parked out the front and driven by an unknown person. His wife is in the front seat. As the car leaves I see that the whole side is transparent, and the roof has been ripped off, leaving jagged black strips of metal hanging down. My lover sits rigid in the back seat, staring blankly ahead as though he can no longer see, or feel, or think. I remain rigid and senseless inside the shop.'

The symbolism here is also fairly transparent. 'Jenny S'

explains: 'This dream occurred after a particularly painful affair and symbolizes the despair and anguish and loss I felt when he said that he couldn't see my anymore.'

Here is one more of her dreams because it shows how interpretation can sometimes lead people to take drastic action, and because its main symbol is a snake. A lot of the letters I got did have snakes in them, though always as symbols of something frightening rather than phallic. Of course, with Freud's theory of distortion, censorship and opposites used for disguise, this may be misleading. 'Jenny S's' dream was set in the lounge room of her parents' home:

'My daughter is lying on the rug watching television, and as I move towards her I am suddenly aware of a flickering in the far corner. To my horror I see a bright orange and red cobra snake weaving and hissing at me, its watery, translucent eyes firmly fixed on me. I am temporarily numbed by the threat it poses, and yet I know that I must save my daughter from this terrible snake. I throw my body across my daughter to protect her, and as I do so the snake begins spitting venom, and I feel the slimy spray projected on to me. But I know that I have beaten the snake and saved my daughter.'

'Jenny S' comments: 'This dream happened when I was having analysis to overcome problems of my relationship with my mother (the snake). It seems that there is a "generation pattern" in my family going back to my great-grandmother where there is an intense relationship between the mother and the youngest daughter. I was determined to break this chain with my own daughter so that she would not have the hassles in her life that I had. As a result of all this, I have virtually severed entirely my relationship with my own mother.'

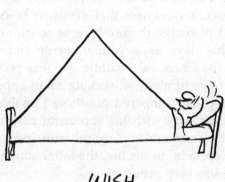

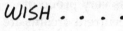
WISH . . . .

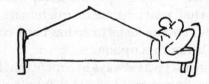
. . . . . FULFILMENT

Some people's nights are invaded by recurring dreams, and they are often terrifying. The content of such recurrent dreams may also be self-critical, revealing, without much analysis, a weakness that needs to be overcome. Freud talked of such a dream. It came to him often and concerned his days as a young doctor and his spell studying at the Chemical Institute. He was pretty hopeless, by his own admission, working as an apprentice in the laboratory. He compared his flawed analysis in the chemistry laboratory with his successful *psycho*analyses later in life, the former being 'an embarrassing and indeed humiliating episode' in his life, the latter something that he, at least, was very proud of.

Obviously recurrent dreams are trying to get an important message across, unsuccessfully. 'Mary B', who, is forty-three, blonde, blue-eyed and with a broad, warm smile, says that getting help to analyse her recurrent dream changed her whole life.

'My marriage broke up a few years ago after almost twenty years,' 'Mary B' explains. 'I was exhibiting severe emotional stress at the time, and an acquaintance recommended that I undergo psychotherapy. During the last three and a half years the dream/nightmare that had been recurring for twenty years or so has been "exorcised", for want of a better description.

'In the dream I was always in a room that had a box-like appearance. Sometimes I feared that I would be drowned or smothered, but usually I simply felt trapped. There was always a door or window in the room, the door being open and the window being accessible to escape, but I never took the "way out". Everyone had gone, and there didn't appear to be anyone left on earth, but I didn't venture out to find them, I just went back to bed with a feeling of utter resignation. On waking from the dream, at times I have experienced absolute terror and have woken screaming.

'In therapy we worked out that the dream meant that people had always taken responsibility for me, and that I had let them. My mother was very domineering, and I married the same sort of man; that was the only environment in which I felt "safe". I had never taken responsibility for myself as that meant disagreeing with people and the fear of being rejected. Because of my over-protected and repressed childhood, I had never learnt to speak up and had become very submissive. I had buried a lot of anger, so therefore suffered a lot of depression. Therapy has taught me to be assertive, non-aggressively, and to establish my own identity and also rebuild my self-image, which was in tatters.

'I am now really "in touch" with my feelings and have grown as a person. The dream/nightmare is no more, the little girl has walked through the door of the room with the courage to take her own life in her hands and speak up for herself. My relationships have improved, and I hope one day to be given the opportunity to make a permanent relationship work.'

Sometimes a nightmare will repeat only once or twice. One such came to me from 'Lucy J', a seventeen-year-old student, whom, it should be said, has never been prone to physical violence. The setting of the dream is explained by knowing that she lived for some years in a farmhouse in England, near which there was an old red-brick barn. This is her dream:

'I was at this barn in the country, and my best friend and I had some whisky, or some sort of spirits. It was a sunny day, and this barn was surrounded by very English looking countryside; in fact, it was almost exactly like Dorset. I cannot recall how I was feeling or what we were

doing. The worst bit of the dream seems to have blocked
out all other trivia. I murdered my best friend and my little
brother by cutting their heads off with an axe. It was
terrible because although I wasn't drunk when I actually
did it, afterwards I had absolutely no recollection of why I
had killed them. I hadn't been angry with either of
them . . . I had no motive in my dream for killing them. I
had put their bodies beneath some rush matting in the
barn so they sort of made a lump. Their heads were also
beneath the rush matting. I think I just wandered around
in a daze for a while, not really knowing what to do or
think. I was in some kind of stupor.

'The next thing I remembered was feeling extremely
relieved and sitting with my best friend just chatting and
smiling. What had happened was that somehow I'd
managed to sew back on her head and that of my little
brother before it was too late. I think I'd realized that I
hadn't actually killed them, and that I could possibly
revive them if I could just sew their heads back on. I don't
know where I found the materials to perform the operation, but I did. The strange thing was that absolutely no
one knew about it, not even my best friend or my little
brother.'

About two weeks later the dream recurred, with some
variations. 'Lucy J' explains: 'This time it didn't involve
my best friend, it involved my other brother, and my little
brother again. I think the setting was much the same,
some remote place. Once again, I wasn't fully in control of
myself. I wasn't drunk or drugged, but I was completely
irrational, though not raving mad. This time I cut both
their heads off with this sort of Arabian knife, and I hid
their bodies and heads. I just didn't know what to do, so
eventually I just left them hidden in the country. There
was some lapse between then and the next part of my

dream, which I don't remember except for this terrible gut feeling, not remorse or fear, more like, "Oh, no, I've done it again."

'In the next part of my dream I was at home and it was about 4 am. I was going to have to tell the adults what I'd done. I stood in the hallway for a while thinking that I shouldn't wake them up, that somehow it would be worse for them to receive such news at such an ungodly hour. Yet, on the other hand, I had this feeling that maybe if I told them now there would be some way of bringing my brothers back to life. Eventually I decided I'd better own up right away, so I went into my parents' room and put the light on, which woke them. I didn't even have to say what I'd done because immediately my Dad sort of sighed and looked really exasperated and said, "Oh, shit. Not again!" And I knew that he knew what I'd done. I felt like an absolute madman, which I suppose I was, and for the first time I started to feel quite guilty, and started crying. The strange thing was that neither of my parents said anything. Dad just looked greatly inconvenienced. But it was terrible all the same. I was standing there crying. I said to them, "Would it make things easier if I killed myself?" Dad said no, that it wouldn't solve anything. So I said they'd better put me in jail or a mental hospital before I did anything else. The second dream was much worse than the first because there was nothing I could do, no way to bring them back to life. I woke up while I was still standing in my parents' room, just waiting for them to react . . .'

'Lucy J' could not offer an interpretation for this dream; all she knew was that it was horrific. But her parents came up with the same interpretation independently, and she agreed that they were probably right. In the six months before the dreams, there had been two shock events. First, one of 'Lucy J's' best friends, a girl only a few months older than herself, had died of a drug overdose. 'Lucy J' had known that she was an addict, but had not discussed this with her parents. She'd convinced herself that her friend 'had it under control'. Secondly, one of her two brothers had been seriously ill, but had survived after his life had been in the balance for a while. The two versions of the dream the parents felt, symbolized 'Lucy J's' feeling of relief (sewing the heads back on) and helplessness (not being able to). There was no malice in the dream or motive for the killings, which seemed to signify the wasteful, senseless death that drug addiction leads to.

The alcohol and the rather annoyed resignation of the parents could indicate a feeling that she bore some responsibility for her friend's death, that somehow she might have prevented it. 'Lucy J's' father felt embarrassed by the light in which he was revealed – exasperated and insensitive.

Naturally, this interpretation could be quite wrong, and if the 'rubbish bin' theorists are correct, it is mindless. But why else would a normally well-adjusted, happy teenager have such macabre nightmares?

Jung warned dream interpreters: 'Every hypothesis about the nature of the dream, its function and structure, is merely a rule of thumb and must be subject to constant modifications. We must never forget in dream analysis, even for a moment, that we move on treacherous ground where nothing is certain but uncertainty. A suitable warning to the dream interpreter – if only it were not so paradoxical – would be; "Do anything you like, only don't try to understand."' Jung ignored his own warning, and remained captivated by dreams all his life. He wrote: 'No amount of scepticism and critical reserve has ever enabled me to regard dreams as negligible occurrences.

Often enough they appear senseless, but it is obviously we who lack the sense and the ingenuity to read the enigmatical message from the nocturnal realm of the psyche.'

Around the world all sorts of research is going on to decipher the enigmatic message. American Professor Calvin Hall has analysed thousands and thousands of dreams, producing such statistical information as 29 per cent of dreams are in colour. Another American, Dr Fred Snyder, has concluded that the most common colour in dreams is green, followed by red. Yellow and blue appear only half as frequently as green. Dr William Dement at Stanford has run experiments to see if outside stimuli can be incorporated by dreamers. He tried a short burst of tone sound, a 100 watt globe flashing in the sleeper's face, and a fine spray of cold water. The three methods were applied to sleepers when their eyeball movements showed that they were in REM sleep. In 9 per cent of cases sleepers incorporated the noise, 23 per cent took in the light flashes, 42 per cent absorbed, as it were, the spray of water.

A more dramatic example of the incorporation of external stimulus was provided by the Frenchman L. Maury, a writer on dreams a bit before Freud last century. Maury was ill in bed, with his mother sitting beside him. In his dream he imagined that he was living during the reign of terror during the French Revolution. He witnessed several people being guillotined after the summary justice of the revolutionary tribunal, then his own turn came. He was cross-examined by Robespierre, Marat, Fouquier-Tinville and others, and, although Maury could not exactly recall for what crime he was sentenced, he was led to the guillotine, surrounded by the dreaded mob and the knitting women. He was bound and led up to the

block. The blade fell, he heard the whoosh, then felt the
sensation of his head and body being parted. Maury woke
in a deep funk, only to find – presumably because his
watching Mum told him – that the top of the bed had
fallen on him as he slept, striking the top of his spine just
where the guillotine blade would have fallen. There are
similar examples, such as that of a man who dreamt that
he had been captured by a band of men, tied up and
staked to the ground through his foot. He woke to find a
piece of straw between his big toe and the next one. A
problem yet to be satisfactorily overcome with such
apparent responses to stimuli is how such a complex tale
could be told in the minute space of time that it would take
for the precipitating event, such as the falling of Maury's
bedhead.

The record for the most embarrassing dream must go to
Cippus, a king of ancient Italy. I came across his tale while
reading one of Montaigne's essays, on the power of the
imagination. King Cippus had been watching the bull-
fights all day, and all night long he continued to see them
in his dreams. So vivid were they that, the story goes,
King Cippus woke in the morning and, to his horror,
found a large horn growing from either side of his
forehead. Such is the power of the imagination (or bull!).

Dr Jim Horne, director of the sleep research laboratory
at Loughborough University in England, wrote in a broad-
ranging article on sleep in the *New Scientist* magazine: 'In
the human adult, a major function of REM sleep may also
be to occupy time, to keep the individual asleep and to
distract the brain from awakening. Dreaming may con-
tribute towards this process by offering stimulation alter-
native to that of wakefulness. It may even be our brain's
natural entertainer: the cinema of the mind.'

Certainly some of the 'movies' are X-rated. They can

also be more frightening than 'Psycho', funnier than 'MASH' and more fantastic than anything to have come out of Disneyland.

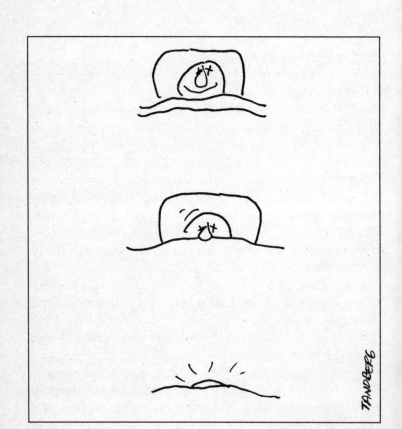

AN A TO ZZZZZZ OF SLEEP

AAAAAAAAAAAAAAAAAAAAAAAAA

Advertising: See entry under murder.

Age: Oldies are associated with doziness, with sitting propped up in a cane chair and catnapping their retirement days away. Oldies are also the biggest consumers of sleeping pills. A paradox. One of the explanations seems to be that older people don't have a lot of the stimulating influences that kept them going earlier in their lives: worry, a job, activities, general haste, energy to burn. At the other end of the scale, prepubescent children in the ten, eleven, twelve age range are reported to be the most wide-awake.

Much research has still to be done on the relationship between age and sleep. Two clues to the difficulties many older people have arise because 40 per cent of them have some form of breathing abnormality during sleep, and they are also more likely than youngsters to have physical movement during sleep. This in turn can lead to daytime sleepiness, and the napping habit, which makes sleep all the less attainable when the next night comes around, and so on. The vicious circle can be redrawn if the person suffers daytime carryover from the sleeping tablets he or she has taken the night before.

American researchers suggest that older people should not let their bedtime creep forward, making nights longer and longer. To help avoid this, some suggest a late morning or early afternoon nap of about thirty minutes, the idea being to improve daytime functioning and to reduce the tendency to go to bed earlier. Obviously long naps late in the day are a bad idea.

Sleep recording surveys have shown that men have more age-related sleep changes than do women. But women complain more about sleep problems and also consume more hypnotic drugs than do men. Possible reasons now being studied include hormonal changes, reduced 'need' in the elderly, possible changes to circadian rhythms as we get older, and the simple fact that boredom and a sedentary life are good reasons to sleep. There's even a Darwinian argument for aged people being light sleepers – they need more time to flee danger.

Alarm clocks: Cave dwellers didn't have them, modern people are ruled by them, and one of the good things about being an oldie is that you need them less and less.

Alcohol: Capping off the day with a snort of port or a belt of brandy has been the traditional way to set oneself up for sleep. But today the nightcap is debunked. It's true that alcohol has the effect of reducing anxiety, and thus promoting sleep, but it also changes the composition, and, most researchers believe, the quality of it. The old law of action and reaction comes into play. The alcohol (and the same is true of sleeping pills) can make you have less anxiety, it can initially prolong sleep, and it can reduce the amount of paradoxical or REM sleep, but when you withdraw it, everything rebounds: sleep is shortened, anxiety increases and there are a lot more dreams through a compensatory REM sleep increase. The extreme case can be seen in what happens to the alcoholic who stops: the DTs. Another illustration of the plus/minus effect of booze is the original recipe for the Mickey Finn that bad guys sought to slip to nice girls: alcohol laced with the sleeping drug chloral hydrate.

Anorexia nervosa: One of the clues to this frightening condition of self-inflicted weight loss is insomnia. It's something to watch for. The insomnia usually decreases with weight gain. A similar thing can happen with depression: weight loss and insomnia increase.

Anxiety dreams: We've all had them, and they can be hell. They're not the same as night terrors (see page 92) because they come out of REM, or dreaming, sleep, while terrors arise from non-dreaming sleep. Freud believed that most anxiety dreams have a sexual basis, even though it may be camouflaged. Dream anxiety attacks are most common from the middle to the second half of the night, when there are more and longer REM periods. Studies have shown that people who suffer them are more artistic, and more likely to suffer mental illness.

Apnea: Greek word meaning breathless, from which we get obstructive sleep apnea syndrome, in which a heavy snorer's upper airway closes, starving the sleeper of oxygen. (See chapter 4.)

BBBBBBBBBBBBBBBBBBBBBBBBBBBBBBB

Barbiturates: Once very popular and dispensed widely to help insomniacs. The fact that they are addictive, have unpleasant withdrawal symptoms and were one of the most effective ways of committing suicide, because of their toxicity in overdose, has meant their virtual disappearance. (See also Von Beyer.)

Benzodiazepines: More popular than barbiturates nowdays, for several reasons, not the least of which is that it is very hard to overdose on them (although they can be fatal if accompanied by alcohol). These modern hypnotic drugs are not physically addictive, as were the barbiturates, but there is a danger with all medicines of psychological dependence. Dr Jim Horne, director of the sleep research laboratory at Loughborough in England has said: 'The best hypnotic is a tablet placed by the side of the bed but not taken.'

Books: There's dispute here: some say a bit of a read is the best way to nod off, others that you shouldn't read in bed. The latter argument is based on the theory that people who have trouble sleeping should not watch television, eat, drink or read in bed. If they do these things, poor conditioning can occur: bed can become associated with just about everything *but* sleep. If you do want to read a lot more about sleep itself, my favourite books on the subject, in order of preference, are: *Some Must Watch While Some Must Sleep*, by William Dement (hard to find in Australia, but some state libraries have a copy in the storeroom); *The Interpretation of Dreams* (Freud, at most good bookshops); *Memories, Dreams, Reflections* (Jung, a biography that he became so interested in his last years that he virtually took it over and made it an autobiography); *The Sleep Disorders* (one of the 'Current Concepts' series published by the US chemical firm, Upjohn. Written by two leading American sleep researchers, Dr Peter Hauri and Dr William Orr, it's very useful once you come to terms with the American obsession with acronyms and jargon). There are more, but many of them are patronizing or boring or both. On the other hand boring books may be just what the insomniac needs. A guest on an ABC books programme once came up with the challenge: 'Show me the person who has actually read right to the end of *Don Quixote*.' This appears to be a cruel insult, for Cervantes is a great writer, but, I've had his tome (all 940 pages of it in the Penguin Classics edition) next to my bed for six months, and I can't get through it. I keep picking it up last thing, plunging in where, I think, I left off, and before you can say 'Sancho Panza', I'm asleep. I thoroughly recommend it.

Bruxism: The fancy name for grinding your teeth in your sleep. This is quite common in children, less so in adults. It's not usually a problem unless the teeth are getting worn down. If this is happening a dentist can supply a plastic or rubber guard for one row of teeth. Teeth grinding is often a bigger nuisance to the bed partner than the perpetrator.

Bulldust: Often used to fill in the gaps where science has failed to find answers. Something to be wary of when discussing sleep. People often wake from a normal night insisting that they 'haven't slept a wink'. Others will say that they don't need any/don't dream/can only sleep with their head pointing north, and so on. Sleep is mysterious, even in the know-all eighties, so it still fosters old wives' tales. And it's worth sometimes pricking the big balloons Freud and Jung blew up. Vladimir Nabokov revelled in this in his novel *Ada or Ardor: A Family Chronicle*, in which his character Van derides the 'secret festerings that the foster quack feigns to heal by expensive confession fests . . .'

CCCCCCCCCCCCCCCCCCCCcccccc

Caffeine: Some sleepers seem to be invulnerable to caffeine, but for most people it does just what some endurance-athletes use it for, that is, it stimulates. People who withdraw from excessive coffee drinking – say ten or more cups a day – can have withdrawal symptoms just like an alcoholic or any other addict. This can mean initially long sleeps, frequent napping, drowsiness and irritability. Some people are particularly susceptible to caffeine, which also lurks in many soft drinks and painkillers. Tea, particularly when it is brewed strong, contains a lot of caffeine; so does cocoa. Sensitivity to caffeine increases with age and prolonged use, so that the coffee you quaffed without bother as a teenager can steadily impinge on sleep as the years pass. For insomniacs who are also coffee and tea lovers a compromise is to stop drinking in the early afternoon, thereafter switching to decaffeinated or non-stimulating herbal brews; you can't have your caffeine and sleep it.

Cataplexy: Nothing to do with flexible cats, but the devastating plunge into zombie-like sleep that hits the unfortunate suffers of the disorder called narcolepsy. In an attack of cataplexy all the muscles go limp, a sufferer can literally fall asleep to the ground. It is sometimes called inappropriate REM sleep, an instant drop from waking to the near-paralysis that is natural in dream sleep. (See chapter 2.)

Censorship: This, according to Freud, is what we do with some of our salacious subconscious thoughts in dreams. We tidy them up, or disguise them. The job of the interpreter is to see behind the façade of censorship (although Jung disagreed with Freud about dreams necessarily having a false front). Freud also felt that the forgetting of dreams involved a degree of resistance to accept their message into the conscious mind, this also being a form of censorship. The prevalence of trivia could also be seen as indicating censorship. He argued that it wasn't right that many dreams were just collections of ephemera, but that we merely sieved out all the important matter. As he put it: 'Superficial associations replace deep ones if the censorship makes the normal connecting paths impassable. We may picture by way of analogy a mountain region where some general interruption to traffic (owing to floods, for instance) has blocked the main, major roads, but where communications are still maintained over inconvenient and steep footpaths normally used only by the hunter.' So next time you think you've been dreaming only of peanut butter sandwiches or parading penguins, think again. One of Freud's interpretations of a censored dream is given in chapter 6.

Cheese: A lot of people believe it gives you bad dreams. There's no evidence for this. The claim may stem from the fact that cheese goes so well with wine, and alcohol *has* been linked to nightmares and other sleep problems.

Cicadas: One of sleep's greatest enemies.

Cigarettes: This alphabetical guide is starting to look like a temperance society manual, but, yes, fags can damage your sleep. Nicotine is the commonest drug of addiction in the world, and we all know that it is a bedfellow of cancer. But inhaled cigarette smoke also stimulates the nervous system, increases depth of breathing and raises blood pressure. It stimulates the release of adrenalin, which, apart from activating us when we should be getting drowsy, is said by some authorities to counteract growth hormones released while we sleep.Long-term use also leads to respiratory problems, which in turn are often blamed for fragmented, unsatisfying sleep.

If you're a coffee-drinking chain smoker with a bent for booze, by now you must be acutely depressed. As an incentive to read on, you may briefly slip down the alphabet to E, for exercise, where you will be pleased to find that most authorities agree that sex and sleep go together very well.

Circadian rhythm: This derives from *circa* (about) and *diem* (day), and is used to describe the biological clock that all life follows, a much more natural timer than the clanging one by the bedside, but one which must be obeyed for successful sleeping. It is described in chapter 1. Jetlag is a good example of what happens to us when our circadian rhythm is out of tune.

Cluster headaches: Some people wake from sleep with agonizing headaches, which seems strange when you think that most of the usual causes should be absent. The reason can be problems with the contraction or dilation of blood vessels in the brain, the former happening during non-REM sleep, the expansion during REM sleep.

DDDDDDDDDDDDDDDDDDDDDDDDDDDD

Death: A lot of people die in their sleep. In many ways they are the lucky ones.

Dement: William C. One of the most articulate and amusing of the modern sleep researchers. He runs the sleep research centre at Stanford University, California. He coined the name REM, for rapid eye movement, or dreaming sleep. As a medical student in the early 1950s, Dement, under the supervision of Dr Nathaniel Kleitman, was one of the first to monitor the movements of sleepers' eyeballs that has come to distinguish dreaming sleep from its opposite, non-rapid eye movement, stages.

Dental dreams: Now you might think dentistry is about as fascinating a subject for dreams as third-year chartered accountancy but, according to Freud, mouth opening can be eye opening. He said in *The Interpretation of Dreams:*

'The meaning of dreams with dental stimulus, which I often had to analyse in patients, escaped me for a long time because, to my surprise, there were invariably too strong resistances against their interpretation. Overwhelming evidence left me at last in no doubt that in males the motive force of these dreams was derived from nothing other than the masturbatory desires of the pubertal period.' He cites two rather unsavoury examples of dental dreams involving a young man with homosexual tendencies having a night out at the opera in one dream, being tied up with silk cloths in the other. In both cases he lost various teeth in the course of the dreams. The link between teeth and sexy dreams may be obscure to some, but Freud partly explains it through the device already mentioned: censorship. He says: 'It may puzzle us to discover how dental stimulus has come to have this meaning. But I should like to draw attention to the frequency with which sexual repression makes use of transpositions from the lower to an upper part of the body. Thanks to them it becomes possible in hysteria for all kinds of sensations and intentions to be put into effect, if not where they properly belong, in relation to the genitals, at least in relation to other, unobjectionable parts of the body.' Given this, it's strange that there aren't more good dentist jokes. The only one I know is the limerick, which I now realize Freud would have enjoyed:

> There was a young girl from Rome
> Who went to the dentist alone
> In a fit of depravity
> He filled the wrong cavity,
> Now she's nursing her filling at home.

Depression: Poor sleep is one of its symptoms; ironically deprivation is one of its cures. In recent years it has been shown that some people suffering endogenous depression (that is, the sort that comes from within, perhaps through some chemical imbalance, rather than depression caused by reaction to circumstances) improve their mood and performance for a few days after a sleepless night. No one quite knows how this therapeutic effect comes about, but some hospitals overseas now use deprivation to treat depressed patients. Clearly it has its limits, but it has been shown to be useful as a stop-gap in the time it takes anti-depressant drugs to start working, which can be some weeks. In one experiment, in 1975, endogenously depressed patients were woken every time they went into REM sleep. This was found to be nearly as effective in treating the depression as was amitriptyline (Tryptanol, Elavil, Saroten, Laroxyl, etc.) Awakenings from non-dreaming sleep had no such beneficial effects.

Drugs taken to treat depression can interfere with sleep at night and increase sleepiness and drowsiness during the day; often they are lifesavers, but there can be difficult adjustment periods while dosage and individual reaction are fine-tuned by the prescribing doctor.

Reactive depression linked to a sudden unpleasant twist in life's path – a death in the family, bankruptcy, a court case, a long-running political battle in the office, a black sheep – usually disrupts sleep until the issue is resolved. Early awakening, with inability to get back to sleep, is common. Although genuine grief has to be lived through and supported, most sleep authorities recommend problem solving rather than pill popping.

Given that depression is estimated to affect at least 10 per cent of people once or more during their life, it must rank as one of the most common sleep disturbers.

Deprivation: it can be a good thing. As secret police around the world know, sleep deprivation can also loosen

the bravest of tongues. It used to be thought that
deprivation of REM sleep was a certain road to madness,
mainly because prolonged wakefulness can lead to hallucination. But there is less support for this theory today.
Going without sleep has long been a challenge for
fundraisers and university students, the record being held
by a young American called Randy Gardner. (See chapter
3.) Some researchers believe that sleep is merely a
conditioned response, not much more than a Darwinian
device to keep a low profile in a dangerous world. On this
theory, deprivation may one day show that we don't
really *need* to sleep at all. For those of us who are
bedophiles (not to be confused with the near homonym)
the concept is about as attractive as nuclear war.

Diaries: People with troubled sleep should keep them. If
you present yourself to a doctor with a written record of
sleep duration over a long period, and a subjective
assessment of how you felt physically and mentally after
each sleep, the doctor is far less likely to be dismissive and
to be writing out a prescription before you've finished
saying what's wrong. If you happen to be referred to a
doctor specializing in sleep disorders, or to a sleep
laboratory, a diary is essential. If you cheat in recording
sleep times, you're cheating yourself.

Dream diaries are another good idea for people who
want to keep in touch with their subconscious. Apart from
any use as a tool for treatment, they can be good fun to
reread and reflect upon. Unless a dream is captured
quickly on paper (or using a tape recorder), it is likely to
fade away fast. The difficulty with dream diaries is that as
soon as the conscious mind is back in control – which it
has to be to some degree just to note down the dream –
there is a risk of censorship, upgrading and slipping in
links and associations that were not really there. Maybe a

solution is to restrict recording to left-hand pages and any interpretation to right-hand ones. For those whose dreams are too hot to leave lying on the bedside table, padlocked diaries can be bought.

Diet: Food and drink affect sleep as much as they do any other physiological functions. There's an argument that the modern obsession with being thin and verging on emaciated is a strong cause of poor sleep. The other exteme, obesity, however, has been well and truly implicated in sleep disturbance, particularly through snoring.

Surveys in hospitals have associated weight loss with shorter, more fragmented sleep and weight gain with longer, uninterrupted sleep. (One extreme is indicated in anorexia nervosa, mentioned earlier in this section.) The same has been shown in the laboratory with rats; fed less they sleep less. Again this can be linked to the survival instinct. The lion in the jungle curls up and has a kip after he's filled his belly. Darwin's law could also be called the survival of the fattest. In one experiment, cats, the most expert of sleepers, were given milk or fat directly into their duodenum, bypassing the gullet. Their sleep was observed to improve, although the exact cause of this could not be explained. (See the entry for milk.) Obviously hunger is a cause of arousal in all animals, so if you go to bed starving there's a fair chance that your belly will rumble you awake. For this reason, many sleep researchers accept the old bedtime snack theory. One person's snack is another's banquet, but it doesn't make a lot of sense to eat like Bacchus before bed. In the 1930s two American doctors compared people's sleep after they'd had a bedtime snack of cereal and milk and after they'd eaten food that was difficult to digest. Measuring the number of body movements during the night in each case, they found, not surprisingly, that the former had less restless sleep than the latter.

Post-prandial drowsiness is likely to decrease markedly now that the federal government has killed off the expenses lunch. We've all felt that beautiful, if often unrequited, desire for a siesta after a big lunch. This can be called the sated fat-cat syndrome, relaxation and drowsiness being by-products of food, drink and friendship. Everyone should do it now and then, even if it means blowing the housekeeping, or, as the siesta-loving Spanish say, 'throwing the house out the window'. Like all good things, you can have too much of it. See also entries under caffeine, obesity and tryptophan.

Direction: The point of the compass to which your head aims when you sleep has been claimed by some to be of vital importance. Napoleon, for instance, is said to have refused to bed down unless his feet were pointing north. A report of an Indian science congress in Bihar State in 1984 quoted advice that people should avoid sleeping with their heads pointing north, but should go for an easterly direction. The Press Trust of India quoted Dr Sarada Subramaniam, professor of physiology at Madras Medical College, as saying that minute magnetic disturbances on Earth could produce big changes in the brain's electrical behaviour. This also affected the biochemical fluids of people sleeping with their heads to the north. Dr Subramaniam was reported to have said these folk could suffer confusion, irritation and a sense of ill health. Eastward pointers were said to enjoy a 'calm and blissful feeling'. It was not explained what happens to the sleep of southerly or westerly pointers.

Dreams: The 'royal road to the unconscious' or 'a load of rubbish'. It's all in the rapid eye movements of the beholder. (See chapter 6.)

Driving: Does not go well with sleeping. The two combined are a significant factor in our road toll. Monotony, warmth and comfort are all conducive to sleep, and all are found on long car trips, particularly at night or after a long day. Getting out and having a walk, even if it's only a few circles around the car, can help. But before the head starts to nod and the car starts to drift at 100 kilometres an hour, a roadside sleep is essential.

Driving also seems to figure in lots of people's dreams. One dreamer's driving exploits and a psychologist's view on what driving dreams can tell us are given in chapter 6.

Drugs: Apart from the ones that we take voluntarily and which have a detrimental effect on sleep – such as alcohol, caffeine, nicotine – there are the ones touted by chemical companies for those who complain of difficulty sleeping or staying awake. Those who argue in favour of hypnotic sleeping pills claim that the modern ones are short-lived in the body, are hard to overdose on, are less likely to lead to rapid tolerance than the old drugs were, and that very low dosages are effective. The most popular ones nowadays are the benzodiazepines (see separate entry). The arguments against drugs are many, the main ones being psychological dependence, dosage difficulties and daytime carryover.

Many doctors will prescribe a sleeping pill to 'break the cycle', the vicious circle of worrying about sleep stopping you sleeping, and so on. And it's true that some modern drugs seem to be more selective and have fewer side-effects than their predecessors. The effective dose of the now superseded chloral hydrate, for example, was often 1 gram; for one of the newer benzodiazepine hypnotics called triazolam, the active amount of drug can be 0.125 milligrams.

A lot of doctors prefer non-drug treatment of sleep disturbances, and psychologists will claim that behavioural solutions are less risky than the pharmacist's bag of tricks.

EEEEEEEEEEEEEEEEEEEEEEEEEEEEEEEEEEEEEE

Earplugs: Well worth a try if you're living near traffic or are a shift worker whose sleep must compete with household noise. The wax ones that shape to fit are best, although they do take a bit of getting used to. It's a help if you can lip read.

Ellis, Havelock: There have been thousands of verses and clever lines written about dreaming and sleep, but his is one of the very best: 'Dreams are real while they last. Can we say more of life?' Havelock Ellis, like Freud, was something of an authority on sex. The two men (both of whom died in 1939) corresponded. Havelock Ellis's main work was *Studies in the Psychology of Sex.*

Enuresis: Bedwetting at night is something we all do at first. Girls grow out of it quicker than boys; some people never do. There are various drug and behavioural approaches to its treatment. (See chapter 5.)

Environment: Noise, heat, humidity, comfort, all are obviously relevant to sleeping. Earplugs, air conditioning and a good bed with soft sheets are equally obvious answers. The psychological environment can be a problem, particularly where going to bed immediately becomes associated in an insomniac's mind with *not* sleeping. Many psychologists advise that people with sleep problems should take more care over their environment, should treat the bedroom with more respect. They suggest not eating, drinking, reading the paper, watching television in bed, only sleeping. You keep yourself right away from that special place until Morpheus is just about to gather you. Thus the association is made and reinforced: bed = sleep. For some, even lovemaking may be better done elsewhere.

Which brings us to emotional environment. Clearly if

the two halves of the marital whole are poised precari-
ously on the outer edges of the double bed, absolutely
determined not to have physical contact with *that* low-
down rat, sleep will not descend as the gentle dew from
heaven. Swallowing pride is more effective here than
swallowing a sleeping pill. If there is no hope of kissing
and making up, there's an argument for making off – to
the sitting room couch. Or this can be used to refuel the
argument. Which party should get up and go? Marriages
may be made in heaven, but they are often unmade in the
bedroom.

Epilepsy: Some people suffer epileptic seizures only
when they are asleep. The clues may be disturbed
bedclothes, blood on the pillow or a wet bed. Fortunately
the problem is fairly rare. Diagnosis may require electroencephalogram recording and analysis. One 1974 study of
epileptic patients revealed that of 645 sufferers thirty-
eight had seizures only during sleep.

EDS: Excessive daytime somnolence. Often the
unpleasant daytime byproduct of nightly insomnia. It is
also caused by some of the lesser known sleep disorders,
such as narcolepsy. It undoubtedly plays a huge role in
office arguments, marital discord and general crabbiness.
We should all pray that Reagan and Gorbachev don't
suffer from it. (See chapters 2 to 5.)

Exercise: A definite sleep enhancer, if done sensibly.
Athletes have been shown to have more slow-wave, or
deep, sleep on days when they have exercised their bodies
than when they haven't. Mild, regular exercise is also said
to help pregnant women sleep better. It's important not to
charge into heavy exercise if you're overweight and unfit
and getting on in years (this can lead to a permanent
sleep). It also doesn't help if you take strenuous exercise

late in the day because increased heart rate and body temperature take time to return to normal, time enough for you to start worrying about why you're not getting off to sleep. The one exception to this rule seems to be sex. Most authorities thoroughly recommend it, the post-coital glow being that unique blend of physical and mental warmth. The proviso is that selfish, one-sided sex is likely to leave the other party wide awake; frustration and anger are enemies of sleep that can endure into the early hours. Sex's sleep-inducing properties are preached so widely that some researchers advocate masturbation where there is no one to share with. While this is morally offensive to some, it has fewer, physiologically at least, complications than do most drugs. American Dr Murray Banks, who mastered that rare combination of medicine and humour, many years ago said that the only known side-effect of masturbation is a strong right arm.

Erections: Hospital sleep laboratories also record male erections. It must be said that this does not require the nursing staff to sleep with the subject. It's done far more clinically, using strain gauges, which are flexible recording devices that fit over the penis and measure expansion. This is not some sort of sanitized voyeurism (although sleep researchers do refer to erections as 'nocturnal penile tumescence'). During REM sleep normal males have erections. The equivalent vaginal enlargement also happens to women in REM sleep, in both cases irrespective of dream content. Where a man reports sexual impotence, the sleep laboratory will find whether he still has the usual erections in REM sleep. If he does, his impotence is likely to have a psychological cause; if he doesn't, the problem is probably physiological.

Either way, it's worth pointing out that nobody has ever

died from impotence. Those who put potency on too high a pedestal would do well to remember an anonymous poem called 'A Suffolk Sea Song':

Man that is born of a woman
Has very little time to live:
He comes up like a fore-topmast staysail
And down like a small flying jib.

FFFFFFFFFFFFFFFFFFFFFFFFFFFFFFFFFFFFFFFFFFFFFF

Factor S: Also known as sleep factor. This may be the beacon of hope for poor sleepers who do not want to take drugs. Two scientists from Harvard University Medical School, Dr John Pappenheimer and Dr Manfred Karnovsky, found that cerebral spinal fluid taken from goats that had been kept awake had the effect of sending other animals to sleep when it was injected into them. The fluid from the sleep-deprived goats sent cats and rats to sleep for between six and twelve hours after a delay of about two hours. What was the magic ingredient?

The two researchers, who have been collaborating for more than thirty years and were in Australia in 1983 for an international congress of physiologists at the University of New South Wales, spent years trying to isolate Factor S. Eventually they decided that it is made by bacteria in the body. They also found that small changes in the molecular structure of Factor S can alter its role as a sleep inducer, even 'turning it off'. Some people with insomnia may have brain receptors that do not respond to Factor S.

Two Swiss scientists (Monnier and Schoenenberger) had similar success when they took blood from sleeping rabbits and injected it into ones that were awake. The second lot soon went off to sleep.

But a lot more work has to be done on understanding Factor S and trying to synthesize it before it is likely to benefit insomniacs.

Fat: People who are chubby (but not obese) are likely to have better sleep than whose who are really thin. (See entries under anorexia, diet and obesity.)

Flurazepam: A hypnotic drug of the benzodiazepine group (see separate entry), sold in Australia under the trade name Dalmane. It has the attraction that people who use it do not quickly develop tolerance, meaning that it can still induce sleep after regular use for three or four weeks. Against it is a decrease in co-ordination for some users.

Foods: The link between certain foods and sleep is a bit like the claims for aphrodisiacs: unproven. Some swear that cheese produces nightmares, others blame chocolate, and so on. It's probably an individual thing – whatever turns you on, or off. Regularity in meal times is said to improve sleep; eating at, say, 6 pm one day and 11 pm the next is more likely to disrupt it. Greasy fast food at midnight will probably narrow your sleep as well as your arteries. So avoid Freud food!

Conversely hunger pangs can keep you awake or cut short an otherwise good sleep. Moderation with the mouth might mean giving the Mogadon a miss. (See also diet, obesity, milk.)

Freud: His book, *The Interpretation of Dreams*, is a must for the bedside table. If you think you've got sleep problems, wait till you read some of his case histories!

GGGGGGGGGGGGGGGGGGGGGG

Gastroesophageal reflux: Better known as heartburn. People who suffer it shouldn't eat too much before bed.

Rising stomach acids are not conducive to sleep. Antacids can help, so can a couple of bricks under the top legs of the bed, making the best use of gravity.

Genesis: No wonder we have nightmares and sleep problems when man's very first sleep is recorded in the Bible thus (although it does have a happy ending): 'And the Lord God caused a deep sleep to fall upon Adam, and he slept, and He took one of his ribs, and closed up the flesh thereof. And the rib which the Lord God had taken from man, made He a woman, and brought her unto the man.'

Getting up: Doing so at the same time each day, even at weekends, reinforces the sleep-wake cycle. A study of the sleeping habits of university medical students showed that those who regularly got up early had better exam results. (See chapter 1.) All sleep researchers agree that regularity of sleep habits is most important. They discourage the common belief that you can treat sleep like plasticine, raging into the night with the idea that a good lie-in will be adequate compensation. Occasionally we all do it; as a way of life only fools do it. (See also circadian rhythm and rituals.)

Green: This is said to be the most popular colour in which we dream. An American researcher, Dr Fred Snyder, found that red came second. Yellow and blue appear in dreams only about half as often as green. Dr Snyder concluded: 'The broadest generalization I can make about our observations of dreaming consciouness is that it is a remarkably faithful replica of waking life.' Another US sleep authority, Professor Calvin Hall, collected thousands of dreams and devised a method of content analysis to summarize them. One of the findings was that colour appeared in 29 per cent of dreams. A lot of the dreamers who wrote to me said their dreams were a mixture of colour and black and white; a few claimed to dream in full technicolour all the time.

Grinding teeth: More a nuisance for the audience than for the performer. (See entry under bruxism.)

HHHHHHHHHHHHHHHHHHHHHHHHHHHH

Hallucinations: Often appear after a long period of sleep deprivation. Some examples are covered in chapter 3: Randy Gardner, who went eleven days without sleep and had virtually no problems, Peter Tripp, a US disc jockey who became almost paranoid after 200 hours awake, and the unreasonable suspicions that affected sleep researcher William Dement after only forty-eight hours. It was once thought that everyone would go quite mad if they were deprived of dreaming for long enough; nowadays a lot of people disagree with this idea.

Many people have minor, harmless hallucinations just before dropping off or just after waking. The former are called hypnagogic hallucinations, the latter hypnopompic hallucinations. They are not proper dreams, they can be hilarious, or very frightening, particulary when they are accompanied, as in some sleep disorders, by a feeling of total paralysis. (See the discussion of narcolepsy in chapter 2.)

HGH: Stands for human growth hormone. Those who argue that sleep is necessary for physical restoration and recuperation (even though this may seem basic, it is disputed) point to the fact that the pituitary gland in the brain releases a lot more HGH into the bloodstream while we are asleep than while we are awake. It has been found that children with growth problems respond better to injections of HGH before bedtime than if they are given it after breakfast.

Hypersomnolence: excessive sleepiness. Some people are just terribly sleepy all the time. Unlike sufferers of narcolepsy (see separate entry), they can, with great effort, fight sleep off, but if there's no real need to they can sleep for twenty-hour stretches. Hypersomnolence may sound like bliss to an insomniac, but it's not. Sufferers have the added disadvantage of not feeling particularly refreshed when they do eventually wake up. Very little is understood about hypersomnolence. The disorder usually strikes first in the late teens or early twenties.

Hypnosis: Some claim great success using it to treat insomnia. It can also be used to treat underlying causes, such as sexual problems and irrational fears. An advantage is that it doesn't have the side-effects of many drug treatments. A doctor in Adelaide who specializes in hypnotherapy and treatment of allergies wrote to me: 'My wife is an insomniac, and I have tried various things to help her, including a machine from Germany that produces electrical "square waves". It did not impress me. Negative ionizers are also *claimed* to help. I have used hypnotherapy with good effect in quite a few patients but cannot recall any controlled trials. It has been established, however, that teaching relaxation is more rapidly effective under hypnosis, and this helps people to sleep naturally. The most effective hypnotic for me is to attend an after-lunch scientific meeting where the lights are dimmed, to show slides!'

Impotence: (See entry under erections.) Sleep laboratories can be useful in determining whether the cause is physiological or psychological. A female chauvinist pig once re-wrote the title of the old song 'A Good Man is So

Hard to Find' to 'A Hard Man is So Good to Find'. But at least there is no medical evidence that impotence causes blindness.

Insanity: Dreams, and insanity have so much in common that people have always sought a connection. Charles Dickens was struck by the similarity one night as he stood outside the high walls of Bethlehem Hospital mental asylum in London. He wrote: 'Are not all of us outside this hospital, who dream, more or less in the condition of those inside it every night of our lives? Said an afflicted man to me when I was last in a hospital like this, "Sir, I can frequently fly." I was half ashamed to reflect that so could I . . . by night. Said a woman to me on the same occasion, "Queen Victoria frequently comes to dine with me and her majesty and I dine off peaches and macaroni in our nightgowns . . ." Could I refrain from reddening with consciousness when I remembered the amazing royal parties I myself had given (at night), the unaccountable viands I had put on the table, and my extraordinary manner of conducting myself on these distinguished occasions? I wonder that the great master who knew everything, when he called Sleep the death of each day's life, did not call Dreams the insanity of each day's sanity.'

Dream interpreters, while agreeing with Dickens that the stuff of dreams *appears* to be quite bonkers, argue that it is no more than a foreign language that needs to be learned.

Insomnia: Inability to sleep. There are scores of causes, fewer solutions (See chapter 3.)

Inspiration: A lot of great thinkers have claimed that their bright ideas or solutions to problems came to them during dreams. Kekulé, the discoverer of the structure of the benzene molecule, got his flash of brilliance while dreaming of entwined snakes. The sewing machine was also 'dreamt up', as was the plot for Robert Louis Stevenson's *Dr Jekyll and Mr Hyde*. (See chapter 6.)

Interpretation: Dreams, being such ephemeral things, are hard to dissect as science would wish. It has been claimed that women are better at interpreting dreams than men, and that their dreams are more descriptive. Men are said to dream more of action, whereas women can recall, say, the colour of a dream character's hair, the pattern on a dress. My wife frequently recalls in her dreams smells that go back to her childhood . . . people, their clothes, the odours of a passageway or her mother's kitchen, a garden. She once dreamt that we'd spent a night on Bali or Fiji and in the morning the fragrance of a redolent tropical night still lingered with her. (This dream would certainly agree with Freud's wish fulfilment theory. We've never been to Bali, Fiji or any island paradise, as she keeps telling me!)

It is dangerous to generalize about dream content and the sexes' ability to interpret, but it's interesting that more than 90 per cent of the people who wrote to me about their dreams were women. Maybe more women write letters than men do. Those who find dream interpretation interesting should read Freud and Jung. Apart from their theories, the story of their own relationship would make a far more gripping television saga than 'Dallas' or 'Dynasty'.

Irritability: Lack of sleep is a prime cause. As a kid I often heard my mother explaining behind her hand to her friends that her badly behaved son was a bit 'T and C'. For a long while I didn't know the meaning, suspecting that it was a mysterious medical complaint, one of those unintelligible disorders such as AC-DC, or an imperative such as POQ, not to mention MYOB. In time it dawned on me that T and C stood for tired and cross. How much nicer the world would be if people slept better! Wouldn't it be great to be able to have access to both objective and subjective sleep studies on, say, the Ayatollah Khomeiny, Margaret Thatcher, Lindy Chamberlain, Ronald Reagan, Lionel Murphy, Norm Gallagher . . .?

JJJJJJJJJJJJJJJJJJJJJJJJJJJJJJJJJJJJJJJ

Jerks (human): Try to avoid them. They're bad for waking and sleeping (especially if you wake up with one next to you after 'sleeping' with them rashly).

Jerks (hypnic): These are less harmful. Hypnic jerks are those sudden sharp body movements many people get, usully in an arm or leg, just as they are sliding from being conscious to unconscious. They tend to bring you back from sleep's brink momentarily. They are nothing to worry about, but do sometimes give your bed partner a fright.

Jetlag: A good illustration of what can happen to us when our circadian rhythm is thrown out.

Jung, Carl Gustav: Swiss psychiatrist. At first an acolyte and then an adversary of Freud's. He died in 1961. Like Freud, he believed that great insight could be had from dreams, but he saw them as a much more mystical and spiritual source than did Freud. He said towards the end of his life: 'I early arrived at the insight that when no answer comes from within to the problems and complexities of life, they ultimately mean very little. Outward circumstances are no substitute for inner experience.' (See chapter 6.)

KKKKKKKKKKKKKKKKKKKKKKKKKKKK

Kant, Immanuel: The eighteenth-century German philosopher who, like Dickens, wondered about the connection between sleep and sanity when he wrote: 'The madman is a waking dreamer.'

Keats, John: Less tart than Kant, but oh how beautiful is his 'Ode to Sleep'. It encompasses insomnia, sleeping drugs (opium), death (he died in his mid twenties of tuberculosis), and a common dream symbol (the key), all with such a sadness and grace.

> O soft embalmer of the still midnight
>   Shutting, with careful fingers and benign,
> Our gloom-pleased eyes, embower'd from the light,
>   Enshaded in forgetfulness divine;
> O soothest Sleep! If it so please thee, close,
>   In midst of this thine hymn, my willing eyes,
> Or wait the amen, ere thy poppy throws
>   Around my bed its lulling charities;
> Then save me, or the passed day will shine
>   Upon my pillow, breeding many woes;
> Save me from curious conscience, that still lords
>   Its strength for darkness, burrowing like a mole;
> Turn the key deftly in the oiled wards,
>   And seal the hushed casket of my soul.

If you like reading before sleep, and enjoy the great English romantic poets, many of Keats's other odes ('To Autumn', 'To a Nightingale', 'On a Grecian Urn', 'On Indolence', 'To Melancholy') have a gentle, almost soporific lilt to them. Another poem with a soothing rhythm and full of imagery to feed your dreams is Hilaire Belloc's 'Tarantella': 'Do you remember an inn, Miranda, do you remember an inn . . . ' and so on.

Some poetry, on the other hand, is built on imagery that is almost guaranteed to stimulate your senses and impinge on sleep. Blake's 'Tiger, tiger, burning bright in the forests of the night . . . ', for example, may fill your dreaming head with piercing yellow feline eyes. And the overwhelming raunchiness of Dylan Thomas's wonderful 'Lament', in which he careers through the sexual stages of man, is no nocturnal lullaby. It is sure to make you have what might be called a Freudian sleep. In the third verse of 'Lament' Thomas gives sleep a mention, with grandiloquent dismissiveness:

> Oh, time enough when the blood creeps cold,
> And I lie down but to sleep in bed,
> For my sulking, skulking, coal black soul!

A Welshman would argue that Keats and Thomas exemplify the differences between the two races.

Keys: Freud read a lot more into keys than did Keats. He saw them quite clearly as phallic symbols, which fitted nicely with his opinion that a room in a dream usually represents a woman. Freud did not say that whole dreams were symbolic of whole situations in life, but he was emphatic that parts of dreams were symbols for parts of reality. As he explains it is his *Interpretation of Dreams:* 'All elongated objects, such as sticks, treetrunks and umbrellas (the opening of these last being comparable to an erection) may stand for the male organ – as well as all long, sharp weapons, such as knives daggers and pikes. Another frequent though not entirely intelligible symbol of the same thing is a nail file – possibly on account of the rubbing up and down. Boxes, cases, chests, cupboards and ovens represent the uterus, and also hollow objects, ships and vessels of all kinds. Rooms in dreams are usually women; if the various ways in and out of them are represented, this interpretation is scarcely open to doubt. In this connection interest in whether the room is open or locked is easily intelligible . . . there is no need to name explicitly the key that unlocks the room.'

LLLLLLLLLLLLLLLLLLLLLLLLLLLLLLLLLLLLLLLLLLLLLLLLLLLLLLL

Latent dream content: the meaning behind what often appears to be mumbo-jumbo. The latter is called the manifest content. Freud's never-say-die argument that all dreams represent wish fulfilment relies heavily on finding the latent lurking beneath the manifest. Thus what appears to be an unpleasant dream (Freud quotes figures from an 1896 survey that purported to show that 57.2 per cent of dreams are disagreeable and only 28.6 per cent are pleasant, with no description for the remaining 14.2 per cent) may be disguised wish fulfilment. He said that even the most apparently superficial and trivial dreams have a significant latent content. 'We do not allow our sleep to be disturbed by trifles', Freud decreed, adding that dreams with what appears to be innocent content turn out, on analysis, to be 'wolves in sheep's clothing'. (See chapter 6.)

Legs: These can be a problem during sleep, although it is not suggested that they be removed surgically. Sometimes they will jerk just before we descend into unconscious sleep (see entry under jerks, hypnic), but for some sleepers they will regularly twitch throughout the night. This is an annoying disorder, often more for the bed partner than the twitcher. It is called nocturnal myoclonus, and is discussed in chapter 2.

Limits: People who want good sleep should set them, both for how late to stay up before hitting the sack, and how long to stay in it once they are there. The arguments for early rising (see entry under getting up) are as important as turning in regularly at a reasonable hour. Limits also need to be set for children on how long they can try to produce spurious reasons for staying up, or getting up once they've been, in that unfortunate phrase, 'put down'. Limits also need to be set for the amount of time they are left crying in the cot before being 'rescued'. Bed and sleep mean separation from parent, a figure of love and protection. Children do need some reassurance that you'll still be there in the morning, and that the boogeyman won't get them. But parents need peaceful sleep too. (See also entry under tucking in.)

Luggage: If you happen to have been carrying a case in your dreams, believing that this was an innocent thing to be doing, Freud's contemporary, Wilhelm Stekel, said that the luggage one travels with represents a load of sin that weighs one down. Freud said luggage stands for 'an unmistakable symbol of the dreamer's own genitals'. Some people think Freud was a hard case.

MMMMMMMMMMMMMMMMMMMMM

Mattresses: People who can afford a Rolls-Royce may choose a lumpy bed. But it's really a question of what the sleeper likes, or has become accustomed to. Experiments do show that people who sleep on a hard board have more movements during the night, more awakenings, and more stage-one sleep than do those who bed on softer surfaces. But there is plenty of evidence that normal sleepers are not greatly affected by the kind of mattress they use. Apart from those who need them for orthopaedic reasons, fantastically expensive 'wonder' beds, including waterbeds, have not been shown to enhance sleep, despite what the ads may say.

Meditation: Whatever turns you off. A lot of people swear by it.

Memory: It's said by some that dreams are hypermnesic, that is, our subconscious memory will dig up things from childhood that in waking life we have 'forgotten'. (See also the entry under interpretation.)

Milk: Does a hot milk drink at night, alone or accompanied by a light snack, promote good sleep? The quality of sleep is hard to measure objectively, but one accepted method is to record the number of movements a sleeper has during the night, on the assumption that restlessness means bad sleep. In the 1930s two American doctors (Laird and Drexel) compared the effects of cornflakes and milk with hard-to-digest snacks, and there was less movement during sleep with the former. In America, Dr Nathaniel Kleitman tried all sorts of bedtime snacks and drinks on sleepers. He found that Ovaltine before bed, whether with water or milk, led to the fewest night moves. Professor Ian Oswald, of the Edinburgh University sleep research centre, tried another proprietary drink made from milk and cereal, Horlicks. He used sixteen volunteers and various control substances, such as an inactive 'folk remedy capsule', plain milk, and a flavoured brew that had no milk or cereal products but which contained the same fats, carbohydrates, protein and calories as Horlicks. The result was that Horlicks emerged the winner, but not by an amazing margin. Professor Oswald's conclusion was that going to bed desperately hungry is not good for sleep. But then going to bed engorged isn't either. He felt that a bedtime routine, with or without a milk drink, was probably the most important thing. The reason why there has been so much interest among researchers in the possible benefits of milk is a substance called tryptophan. (See separate entry.)

Money: Freud said: 'Dreams with an intestinal stimulus throw light in an analogous fashion on the symbolism involved in them, and at the same time confirm the connection between gold and faeces which is also supported by copious evidence from social anthropology.' So who needs the Midas touch!

Murder: Inability to get to sleep has led people to commit it (battered babies, for instance). That's deadly serious. The Viennese satirist Karl Kraus, a contemporary of Freud's, complained about sleep itself being murdered by advertisers. The caustic Kraus was the antithesis of an ad man. He ran and wrote his own newspaper called the *Torch*, and once said of it: 'I and my public understand each other very well: it does not hear what I want to say, and I don't say what it wants to hear.'

All newspaper journalists have a queasy relationship with advertising, but Karl Kraus found that his invaded his sleep. 'Mercantilism has been bold enough to use even the threshold of our consciousness as a plank,' he moaned. 'The everyday world did not offer room enough, and so the horrible possibility, the very thought of which made us choke, has become a reality: advertising faces have been used for those hypnagogic figures that surround our beds when we are half asleep. And since there are also hypnagogic sounds, auditory hallucinations to which drowsy scenes are prone, they have chosen – I shudder to think of it – all those slogans and summonses which fill our consciousness by day.'

Kraus fantasized about the extent to which advertising's invasion of sleep could go: 'And since life is surging around my bed of pain in such profusion, offering all the conveniences and all the automatic joys that can be obtained at this point of time, a gun dealer notices I no longer know what is going on, and drowns out the din with his own slogan: "Be your own murderer!" '

And Kraus died in 1936, when the Hidden Persuaders were mere amateurs!

NNNNNNNNNNNNNNNNNNNNNNNNNNNN

Naps: Can be an important aid to alertness while awake and to gaining some control over night-time sleep, particularly among older people. Sleep authorities refer to strategic napping, having short sleeps at certain times of the day. (See entry under age.)

It's true that you can't sleep all day and then expect to keep it going most of the night, but a lot of sleep researchers disagree with Friedrich Nietzsche, who wrote in *Thus Spake Zarathustra*: 'No small art it is to sleep! It is necessary for the purpose to keep awake all day.'

Narcolepsy: A sleep disorder in which sufferers literally fall asleep. It is characterized by cataplexy (a sudden and sometimes complete loss of muscle tone that has the effect of paralysis) by excessive daytime sleepiness, and hallucinations. It must rank as one of the cruellest disorders known to mankind because one of the prime causes of an attack is excitment or laughter; the worst thing you can do for a narcoleptic is to tell him or her a good joke. (See chapter 2.)

Need: It might seem self-evident that we all need to sleep, but some sleep researchers don't think so. One goes so far as to say that it's only a matter of time before a happy, healthy non-sleeper is found, or produced by scientists deactivating the brain's sleep centres. It is true that some people need far less sleep than others. There are two well-documented cases in Australia of men who needed only three hours or less a night, and in England a sprightly retired nurse showed that she consistently got

by on about an hour a night. She did not like the word
'insomnia'; she felt sorry for people who aimed for eight
hours a night because they wasted so much time. (See
chapters 1 and 3.)

Nightmares: The distinction needs to be made between
anxiety dreams and night terrors. The former arise out of
REM, or paradoxical, sleep and are proper dreams that can
wreck your night. (The word is derived from the Sanskrit
word *mara*, which means destroyer.) The horror of
nightmares is often magnified because in dream sleep the
body is virtually paralysed (that's why it's called paradoxical, because your mind, and eyeballs, are really on the
move, but your body is as though frozen). This sensation
of paralysis just on waking can give that feeling of being
trapped, of being unable to escape whatever horror is
upon you. Freud claimed that anxiety dreams in particular
could be traced back to sexual causes. Many disagree with
him.

Night terrors are different in that they do not arise out
of REM sleep, but from non-dreaming, or non-REM
stages. They also tend to have a much simpler message
than a full-blown dream. The vision in a night terror may
be of, say, a pair of 'evil' hands getting closer and closer to
your throat to strangle you, or the walls of the room
steadily moving in to crush you. One such case is
described in chapter 5. Night terrors mainly affect young
children, who may awake screaming, but sometimes they
carry over into adulthood. Often the child will have no
memory of the terror next morning, not even that they
woke screaming. So parents often suffer more from them
than do the sleepers. There is no known cure for them.
Neither is there for nightmares, although it is known that
certain things are likely to induce them: depression,
anxiety, alcohol. Television violence is also probably a

culprit. I have no real evidence for this other than logic,
and my younger sister's accusing me of having provoked
her very first nightmare by making her watch 'King Kong'
when I was babysitting her.

Noise: Some sleepers handle it better than others.
Expected noise, such as an always-loud air-conditioning
system or a fridge that has a heavy nocturnal hum, can
often be adjusted to. It can even be depended upon, as by
the miller who couldn't sleep without the background
noise of the grindstones. Random noise, such as a police
siren or someone hammering on the front door, is much
more likely to break sleep. Noise that is expected but
which is not regular – for example, the sort that people living on an aeroplane flightpath experience – is handled
better by some people than others. A survey of 6,000
people living near Heathrow Airport, London, showed
that those who felt angry about the noise of planes had
more sleep problems than those who heard the same
noise but took it as a fact of life.

There have been lots of experiments in which various
sounds at various volumes have been played to sleepers,
particularly to see how this outside stimulus can be
incorporated into dreams. In one test, sleepers were
played recordings of their own voice during REM sleep, at
a level not loud enough to wake them. Then they were
played other people's voices at the same volume. It was
found that the sleeper's own voice led to the main
character in the dream being active, assertive, indepen-
dent and helpful. The character became far more passive
when another person's voice was played.

An experiment by students at Stanford University sleep
research centre in 1971 tried a similar test using lots of
familiar sounds – a rooster crowing, a bugle playing
Reveille, a barking dog, a steam train, traffic, and a speech

by Martin Luther King. Subjects were given ten-second bursts during their REM sleep. The students said their survey showed that in just over half the experiments the noise played had been incorporated into the sleeper's dream in some way. The sound of the steam train turned out to be the most effective stimulus, the traffic noise the least.

There are no easy answers for tackling noise, although double glazing, good sound insulation and earplugs can help. In most Australian states, environment protection authorities and various parliamentary statutes can be invoked where uncaring humans (or their pets) are the cause.

OOOOOOOOOOOOOOOOOOOooo

Obesity: Although it is true that weight loss has been associated with insomnia, it's also harder to have good sleep if you're rippling with fat. Hugeness doesn't help your heart, or your breathing.

Obstructive sleep apnea syndrome: This is the condition that can change snoring from a joke to a potential disaster. Sufferers literally stop breathing during their sleep. Often, but not always, it is a bedfellow of obesity, fellow being deliberate rather than discriminatory because it is mainly a male problem. Chapter 4 is devoted to snoring.

Orthodox: Also known as non-dreaming, or non-REM sleep. Roughly 80 per cent of our nights are spent in it. It's not true that we never dream in orthodox sleep, but we are less likely to, and those that we do have are shallower and less detailed than in REM sleep. Some authorities say that orthodox sleep is as important for us physically as dreams may be for us psychically, support coming from it being during orthodox sleep that growth hormone is released into the blood and very little energy is consumed. An extension of the latter is the extreme variety of orthodox sleep used by some animals – hibernation.

PPPPPPPPPPPPPPPPPPPPPPPPPPPPPPPPPPP

Paradoxical: Another name for REM sleep. This is the stuff of dreams. Its name comes from the fact that during it our bodies are leaden, with almost no muscle tone, yet our minds are alive with bizarre, beautiful or bad thoughts, and our eyeballs frequently dart from side to side beneath our closed lids. The amount of blood flow to the brain increases, so does brain temperature. But, in keeping with the paradox, body temperature controls are absent. We don't sweat or shiver in paradoxical sleep.

Paralysis: A brief feeling of it on waking is not uncommon. Sleep paralysis can also be a symptom of the disorder known as narcolepsy.

Parasomnias: The name that lumps together all the disorders other than insomnia and excessive somnolence. (See chapter 5.)

Pillows: Largely a matter of personal preference. The wife of a snoring dentist at Echuca, on the Victoria-New South Wales border, has invented one that is said to do wonders for snorers (and their families) . . . and more than 60,000 of them have been sold. John Steinbeck asked in *Tortilla Flat*, 'What pillow can one have like a good conscience?' (See chapter 4.)

Polysomnography: A way of describing, in many syllables, the art of recording electronically and in other ways, virtually everything a sleeper does.

Pregnancy: Sleep can be elusive during the latter stages of pregnancies because sheer size may make it hard to get comfortable, and the baby may decide to play internal football for half the night. Sleeping drugs or nightcaps are more risky than ever because they can affect the baby, too. Many doctors advise regular, mild exercise – such as walking in the fresh air – and a supportive mattress if backache is a problem. Supportive husbands help, too.

Prophecy: It's great with hindsight; very few bookmakers have suffered bankruptcy through prophetic punters. The case of the English baronet who dreamt that the Titanic would hit an iceberg and sink is often cited. He's reported to have written to newspapers about his dream *before* the event, but to have been scoffed at. When the ship went down, he committed suicide. Sometimes it's hard to distinguish prophecy from coincidence or from reasonable expectation. If you dreamt, for instance, that there was to be a big plane crash in the near future, you'd probably be proved right. So little is known about dreaming that it would be a rash person who would deny the possibility of prophesy.

Certainly Jung didn't. In his book, *Modern Man in Search of a Soul,* he recounted what happened to a friend of his in Zurich: 'He was a man somewhat older than myself whom I saw from time to time, and who always teased me on these occasions about my interest in dream interpretation. I met him one day in the street and he called out to me: "How are things going? Are you still interpreting dreams? By the way, I've had another idiotic dream. Does it mean something to you?" He had dreamed as follows: "I am climbing a high mountain over steep, snow-covered slopes. I mount higher and higher – it is marvellous weather. The higher I climb, the better I feel. I think, if only I could go on climbing like this forever! When I reach the summit, my happiness and elation are so strong that I feel I could mount right up into space. And I discover that I actually can do this. I go on climbing on empty air. I awake in a real ecstasy.''

'When he had told me his dream, I said, ''My dear man, I know you can't give up mountaineering, but let me implore you not to go alone from now on. When you go, take two guides, and you must promise on your word of honour to follow their directions.'

Jung says his friend replied: 'Incorrigible!' and laughed at him before saying goodbye. 'I never saw him again,' Jung said. 'Two months later came the first blow. When out alone, he was buried by an avalanche, but was dug out in the nick of time by a military patrol which happened to come along. Three months later, the end came. He went on a climb accompanied by a young friend, but without guides. An alpinist standing below saw him literally step out into the air as he was letting himself down a rock wall. He fell on to the head of his friend, who was waiting beneath him, and both were dashed to pieces far below.'

A cynic would point out that mountaineering is intrinsically dangerous, that oxygen starvation can make us do funny things. But then . . .

Pyjamas: There are lies, damned lies, and naked statistics. One of the most amazing I've found is that 40 per cent of all American women sleep in the nude, while only 25 per cent of men do (the rest sleep in tops, bottoms, both, or nighties or nightshirts). Would these figures hold true in the Soviet Union (Siberia excluded for obvious reasons), far north Queensland, Glasgow or Gibraltar? And if they do (or don't) what does it mean? Trivia freaks may also like to know the derivation of this strange word: the *py* comes from the Urdu word for leg and the *jamas* from the Hindi one for clothing, time and custom extending them to the upper half, too.

QQQQQQQQQQQQQQQQQQ

Quantity and quality: The former can be pinned down in a sleep laboratory, the latter is far more elusive. It's true that some people need more sleep than others, and that sometimes you can awake from a short nap feeling rejuvenated, yet feel washed out and weary after eight hours in bed. Sleep is said to be 'deepest' during the later stage of orthodox, or non-REM sleep, when delta or 'slow' waves show up on electroencephalogram recordings of brain activity. Apart from the subjective and imprecise method of asking sleepers 'how they feel' when they wake, measurements can also be made of body movements throughout the night. Older people, who generally complain more of poor quality sleep, do have more body movements at night. At the other end of the scale, people refer to 'sleeping like a baby'. It may be that 'poor' sleepers must substitute quantity for quality. In the animal world the giant sloth tops the quantity table, managing to sleep twenty hours in each twenty-four. The domestic cat averages fourteen hours (mice sleep thirteen hours), and the humble horse, along with the roe deer, is the shortest sleeper, getting by on about two hours a day. But then maybe horses have nightmares?

Quiet: One of sleep's best friends. (See entry under noise.)

Quirks: Some people develop quirky habits, or rituals, about their bedtime. If the routine is broken, they can't sleep. One chartered accountant is reported to have been obsessive about folding his clothes neatly before retiring. He had to get out of bed five or six times a night to check the folds and creases. This story may be apocryphal, but it's useful ammunition if your bed partner nags you about clothes being flung on the floor. Just as he/she is

delightfully groggy with sleep, you leap out to pat and
preen your already immaculately folded jeans and T-shirt.
On the other hand, this is probably grounds for divorce.

RRRRRRRRRRRRRRRRRRRRRRRRRRRRRRRRRRRRR

Relaxation: Learning it can markedly increase receptivity
to sleep and reduce the need for hypnotic drugs. Psychologists sometimes refer to relaxation therapy as 'the
behavioural aspirin'. Its opposites – worry, fear, tension,
stress – are among sleep's greatest enemies. In chapter 3
the approaches of two psychologists are discussed:
Michael Young of Sydney and David Morawetz of Melbourne. Both seem to have had a lot of success.

Rebound: The compensation effect, when natural sleep
is interrupted or interfered with. A sleeper deprived of
REM sleep will have a rebound or increased amount of it
for a while when normal sleeping resumes. It was partly
this catching up effect that led some people to believe that
without REM sleep we'd go mad, a view no longer widely
held. There is also a rebound effect from loss of non-REM
sleep. Some sleeping drugs, such as barbiturates, will
suppress REM sleep and cause rebounding. The nastiest
rebound is that suffered by the alcoholic going through
delerium tremens after withdrawing. REM sleep, which
occupies about 20 per cent of the night, shoots up to
almost 100 per cent. It is thought to be this that leads to all
those pink elephants as dream sleep breaks through into
the waking psyche.

REM and non-REM: Rapid eye movement and its opposite,
non-rapid eye movement. Used to describe the two main
types of sleep, REM being the one in which we dream a
lot, non-REM the one in which we dream less. Our nights

are broadly divided into 20 per cent REM and 80 per cent non-REM.

Rituals: Most people have some sort of ceremonial unwinding that makes the transition from vertical to horizontal easier. For example, at 11 pm your favourite television programme has finished, you go downstairs, put out the cat, switch off the lights, check that the stove is not on, fill a glass of water, check the children's bedrooms, go back upstairs, undress, do your teeth, read for ten minutes, set the alarm clock . . . The variety of sleep rituals is endless and individual. Their significance is that, even though we may take them for granted, they are routine signals to shut down. Not having a ritual, or not following it, may be a significant cause of insomnia. Rituals do sound exceptionally dull (it'd be far more fun to be out carousing), but it all gets back to the fact that sleep is not a noxious weed but a fairly delicate plant that needs tending if it's not to wither.

Rubbish bin theory: This is a brave new world idea that equates dreaming with emptying out the mind of useless material, a sort of purging of the cerebral computer. It's anathema to dream analysts.

SSSSSSSSSSSSSSSSSSSSSSSSSSSSSS

Schedule disorders: People who want to sleep by day and wake by night may just be 'night owls' by nature, or they may have what are known as disorders of the sleep-wake schedule. If your biological clock keeps telling you that you are not sleepy until 3 am each day, but your alarm clock keeps telling you you must get up for work at 7 am, you've got problems, not the least of which is that the boss will notice that you spend half the day yawning.

Sleep- wake schedule disorders can be tackled with a non-drug treatment called 'chronotherapy', which is simply a method of resetting you biological clock to more 'appropriate' hours. If you live a self-sufficient life in the jungle, sleep-wake schedule disorders won't be a problem. Chronotherapy is explained in chapter 1.

Serotonin: This is a chemical transmitter to the brain that has often been associated with sleep. It has a relationship with an amino acid called tryptophan (see separate entry), which may act as some sort of trigger and which is found in many foods. Various biochemists are toying with serotonin. One suggestion is that reducing the effects of serotonin blurs the distinction between REM sleep and wakefulness.

Shift work: A survey by the brain behaviour institute at Melbourne's La Trobe University showed that shift workers employed by the State Electricity Commission were more prone to disorders of sleep, digestion and the nervous system than were day staff. The head of the institute, Professor George Singer, suggested various changes for industries that work shifts that interfere with people's normal diurnal rhythms. Among them was that night shifts, or blocks of them, should be followed by twenty-four hours off work and that preferably night shifts should be rostered singly among day or afternoon shifts rather than given in big lumps. He also advocates places for shift workers to nap, an idea that may sound like bludging but which seem less so when you learn that this is what the efficient Japanese car industry does. For those who want to know more about this subject, *Shiftwork and Health* is published by the Brain Behaviour Research Institute, Department of Psychology, La Trobe University, Bundoora, Australia, 3083.

Snoring: Sometimes the foghorn of the night is funny;

sometimes infuriating; sometimes fatal. Chapter 4 is devoted to snoring.

Somnambulism: Sleepwalking. If you wake up with grass between your toes, you've probably been somnambulating. (See chapter 5.)

Sudden infant death syndrome (SIDS): A tragic riddle of sleep that has left many parents devastated. It has been suggested that SIDS is linked to obstructive sleep apnea, but one Australian authority says it appears that 'there is probably not a very strong connection'. (See chapter 4.)

Surf sound sleep inducer: A 'white noise' device that has been used to help some insomniacs, who describe the sound it emits as 'a magnet for my thoughts'. Its effect is being tested by psychologist Michale Young at the University of New South Wales. (See chapter 3.)

Symbols: You can buy dream books that will tell you that going up in a lift symbolizes sexual intercourse, losing a tooth means castration, that armchairs equate with breasts, that woman is symbolized by a house or a sailing boat. Why don't we simply say what we mean in dreams, call a spade a spade? The Freudian answer is that we censor and distort our dreams because we want to repress certain unpalatable thoughts. (See also entry under keys.)

T T T T T T T T T T T T T T T T T T T T T T T T T T T T T T T T T T T T T T T T

Talking: A lot of sleepers fear that they may give away secrets, but most people talk gibberish. Some people who wrote to me said that they apparently conduct reasonably lucid conversations with their bed partners while asleep. It can happen at any stage of the night, often accompanies sleepwalking, and is nothing to worry about.

Temperature: Your body temperature is on an upward curve during the day and a downward one at night. Our abilities – physical and mental – rise and fall with this temperature graph, which means that a night shift worker is more accident prone than a day shift one. During REM or dream sleep the body's normal temperature balancing mechanisms – sweating and shivering – stop working.

The temperature around the sleeper is another matter. Tests on rats show that they sleep best when kept between 30°C and 32°C. Cats have been shown to sleep longest when the temperature is 22°C. For humans, there are indications (such as more awakenings and body movements) that when the mercury is above 24°C sleep is less smooth. A study of people in arctic contitions (from 0°C to 5°C) showed that REM sleep was reduced by about a quarter.

Togetherness: Psychologically, sleeping with a loved one is great, but it may not improve your sleep. There can be roll-into-the-middle problems where one partner is very heavy and the other light (although modern mattresses can compensate for this). In 1969 a study was made of couples who were good sleepers together. Trials on them when they were sleeping apart showed, however, that they got more delta, or deep, sleep, and less REM sleep. Such statistics are nevertheless unlikely to dent the double bed sales figure.

Tucking in: This can be a very important ritual for children, who can come to associate it with security, safety and being loved. It can often provide the full stop to a bed-time song or story.

Tryptophan: Some researchers say that this amino acid found in protein foods promotes sleep through its relationship with a brain transmitter called serotonin (see separate entry). There is a theory that tryptophan is best absorbed when accompanied by carbohydrate. Milk contains tryptophan, cereals contain carbohydrates, thus proprietary bedtime drinks such as Ovaltine and Horlicks, which are made from milk and cereals, really do work. Other researchers think tryptophan has been over-rated. Professor Ian Oswald, of Edinburgh University, has described some of the claims for it as 'based on muddled thinking'.

UUUUUUUUUUUUUUUUUUUUUUUUUUUuu

Ultradian rhythm: This is a smaller biological clock than the twenty-four-hour circadian rhythm (see separate entry). It works on cycles of about a hundred minutes. Our ultradian rhythms produce those peaks and troughs of alertness/drowsiness, appetite/content, calmness/ restlessness during our waking hours. They also govern our REM and non-REM sleep stages.

Useless: Much of the advice handed out on sleep fits into this category. Watch out for it.

VVVVVVVVVVVVVVVVVVVVVVVVVVVVvvv

Vested interests: Some useless advice will come from people who have these. Makers of beds, pillows, blankets, pyjamas, mattresses, hypnotic drugs, over-the-counter preparations and books on sleep . . . they/we all have a vested interest in your wallet as well as your welfare. Morpheus and the Underworld!

Vitamin B6: I once heard at a seminar on dreams that B6 promotes dreaming. But be careful, vitamin freaks are vocal, and sometimes have a vested interest.

Violence: Big doses of it from television, especially for children, wouldn't seem to make sense. In 1964 two scientists divided volunteer children into two groups, showing one lot a bloodthirsty western before bed and the

other lot a romantic comedy. Neither group incorporated
what they had watched into their dreams, although the
dreams of those who saw the violent western were
described as more vivid. While this proves nothing, why
run the risk?

Von Beyer, Adolf: He invented the most
famous/infamous group of sleeping pills so far: the
barbiturates. He did this by combining in his laboratory
malonic acid and urea. The day he arrived at his discovery
was St Barbara's Day (she was the patron saint of artillery
officers) in Berlin in 1864, so he combined Barbara and
urea to get barbiturate. Today 'Barbies' are generally
frowned upon because they're addictive.

WWWWWWWWWWwwwwww

Weather: It can influence sleep as we all know, and as
research has confirmed. More than twenty years ago it
was demonstrated that extremely high and extremely low
barometric pressures could be linked to increasing sleepiness. (See also entry under temperature.)

Wish fulfilment: Freud believed that all dreams were
based on this. Those dreams that on the surface appeared
to be horrific or unpleasant were simply distortions to
cover up wishes – usually sexual – that were repressed.
(See also entry under latent.)

Wool: The country may no longer ride on the sheep's
back, but a lot of Australians are sleeping on it. A study of
the effects of sleeping on wool was reported in the *Medical
Journal of Australia* in 1984. It was done by Associate
Professor Peter Dickson of the College of Administrative
Science in Columbus, Ohio. He photographed nine men
and one women for three nights sleeping in their own
homes on a woollen underlay, then for three nights on a

control mattress without one. All were described as good sleepers. The results showed fewer body movements and much less tossing and turning on the woollen underlay. Apart from the photographic evidence, the subjects all said they felt that they'd slept better the mornings after they'd been on wool. Professor Dickson suggested possible reasons: the woollen pile may have diffused pressure points such as at shoulders and hips; better insulation, giving a more consistent temperature; absorption of sweat; tactile pleasure, even when covered with a sheet. Manufacturers of woollen underblankets also claim that they are successful for people with backache, arthritis and rheumatism. Most Australians will have seen the suave Stuart Wagstaff promoting them on television (but then he also promoted Benson & Hedges cigarettes!).

Worry: Try not to. As the worry graph climbs, so the sleep graph falls. It's better to tackle the root cause of the worry than it is to toss and turn, pop a pill, or bite your partner's head off.

XXXXXXXXXXXXXXXXXXXXXXXXXXXXXXXX

This one's always excrutiating for the compiler of alphabetical lists. Unfortunately, sleep can't be X-rayed. What insomniacs can do is count words starting with X rather than sheep. There are nearly two dozen of them if you include proper nouns. If it doesn't get you off to sleep, it should at least improve your Scrabble score. Or you can always go and have a snooze on your xystus. Every house should have one!

YYYYYYYYYYYYYYYYYYYYYYYYYYYYYY

Yawning: This is sleep's way of letting dinner guests know that their conversation is boring although the true blue bore can usually take even a full-frontal yawn in his or her stride, with something like: 'That reminds me of the time I went down a coal mine in Nottinghamshire wearing thongs. Did I ever tell you about that? No, well, you see . . .'

Yearning: This sometimes produces great poetry (see entry under Keats) but rarely produces sleep. There's an argument that Morpheus is stone deaf.

ZZZZZZZZZZZZZZZZZZZZZZZZZZZZZ

Zeitgebers: 'Time givers' in German. Sleep researchers refer to them when they talk about any of the things that shape our sleep-wake periods and therefore involve our circadian rhythms. An alarm clock is a zeitgeber, so is a meal-time or working, so are sunrise and sunset.

Z, of course, also stands for Zzzzzzzzzzzzzz.

Sweet REM stages!